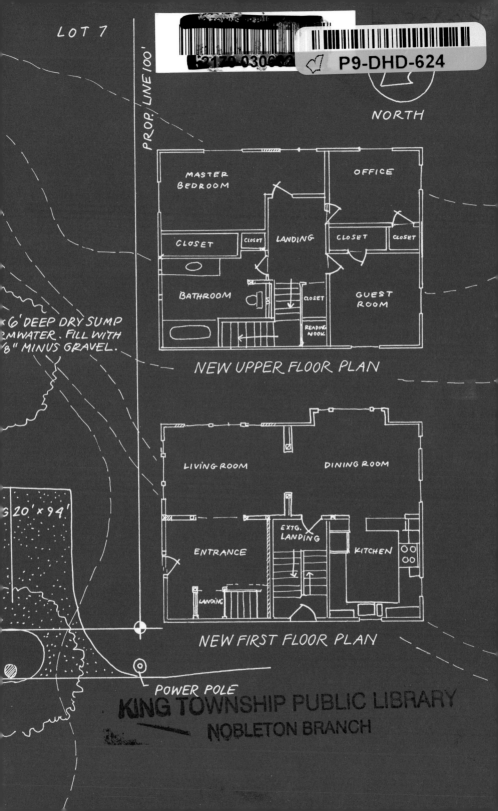

LOT 7

PROP. LINE 100'

P9-DHD-624

NORTH

NEW UPPER FLOOR PLAN

MASTER BEDROOM

OFFICE

CLOSET · CLOSET · LANDING · CLOSET · CLOSET

BATHROOM

GUEST ROOM

CLOSET

READING NOOK

6' DEEP DRY SUMP
RMWATER. FILL WITH
8" MINUS GRAVEL.

NEW FIRST FLOOR PLAN

LIVING ROOM

DINING ROOM

EXTG. LANDING

ENTRANCE

KITCHEN

LANDING

20' x 94'

POWER POLE

KING TOWNSHIP PUBLIC LIBRARY
NOBLETON BRANCH

HOUSE LESSONS

Also by Erica Bauermeister

FICTION

The School of Essential Ingredients
Joy for Beginners
The Lost Art of Mixing
The Scent Keeper

NONFICTION

500 Great Books by Women: A Reader's Guide
with Jesse Larsen and Holly Smith

Let's Hear It for the Girls: 375 Great
Books for Readers 2–14
with Holly Smith

HOUSE
LESSONS

Renovating a Life

ERICA BAUERMEISTER

Illustrations by Elizabeth Person

SASQUATCH BOOKS
SEATTLE

Copyright © 2020 by Erica Bauermeister

All rights reserved. No portion of this book may be reproduced or utilized in any form, or by any electronic, mechanical, or other means, without the prior written permission of the publisher.

Printed in the United States of America

SASQUATCH BOOKS with colophon is a registered trademark of Penguin Random House LLC

24 23 22 21 20   9 8 7 6 5 4 3 2 1

Editor: Hannah Elnan
Production editor: Bridget Sweet
Design: Anna Goldstein
Illustrations: Elizabeth Person
Cover photograph: © Melanie Kintz / Stocksy United

Library of Congress Cataloging-in-Publication Data is available.

ISBN: 978-1-63217-244-0

Sasquatch Books
1904 Third Avenue, Suite 710
Seattle, WA 98101

SasquatchBooks.com

Certified Chain of Custody
Promoting Sustainable Forestry
www.sfiprogram.org
SFI-01268

SFI label applies to the text stock

For Ben

He who loves an old house
never loves in vain.

—Isabel Fiske Conant

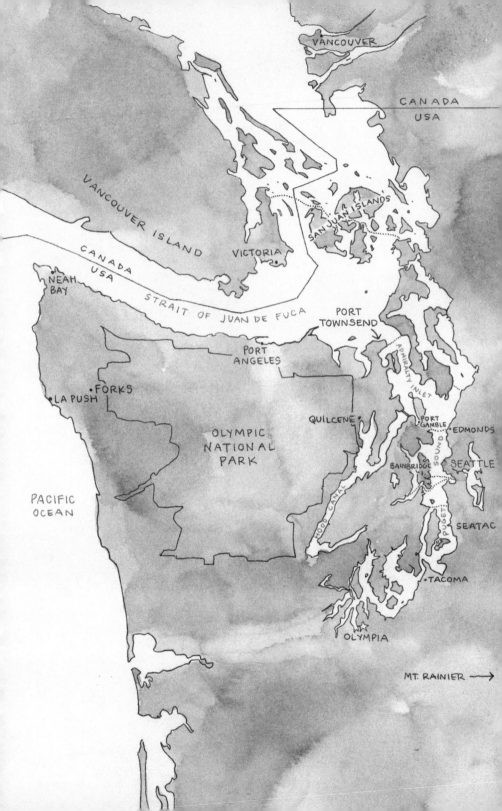

CONTENTS

AUTHOR'S NOTE

THERE IS A TRADITION IN straw-bale construction called a "truth window." A small square is cut out of the plaster surface of the walls, exposing the straw within, so everyone will know what the house was made of. The square can be framed, covered in glass, and sometimes it even has a door—but it is always a snapshot of the construction process, a glimpse into the story of the building.

House Lessons is my truth window. As with any window, it can show only what the builder chooses to frame, the view he or she finds most intriguing. My story is therefore different than what my husband or children, or any of the many other people who were part of our renovation, would write. I leave those stories to them. Because I believe their lives are their own, I have also changed most of their names—and for the sake of narrative flow, I've occasionally conflated several characters or occurrences into one. This is a story, after all.

Come, look inside.

PROLOGUE

THE HOUSE STOOD AT the top of a hill, ensnarled in vegetation, looking out over the Victorian roofs of Port Townsend and beyond, to water and islands and clouds. It seemed to lean toward the view as if enchanted, although we later learned that had far more to do with neglect than magic. The once-elegant slopes of its hipped roof rolled and curled, green with moss. The tall, straight walls of its Foursquare design were camouflaged in salmon-pink asbestos shingles, the windows covered in grimy curtains or cardboard. Three discarded furnaces, four neon-yellow oil drums, an ancient camper shell, and a pair of rusted wheelbarrows lay scattered at odd angles across the overgrown grass as if caught in a game of large-appliance freeze tag.

The yard was Darwinian in its landscaping—an agglomeration of plants and trees, stuck in the ground and left to survive. Below the house, I could just see the tips of a possible orchard poking up through a roiling sea of ivy. In front, two weather-stunted palm trees flanked the walkway like a pair of tropical lawn jockeys gone lost, while a feral camellia bush had covered the porch and was heading for the second story. Someone had hacked away a rough opening for the front stairs, down which an assortment of rusted rakes and car mufflers and bags of fertilizer sprawled in lazy abandon. In their midst, seemingly oblivious to its setting, sat a rotting fruit basket, gift card still attached.

"That one," my husband, Ben, said as he pointed to the house.

"It's not for sale," I noted.

"I know. But it should be, don't you think?"

Our son and daughter, ten and thirteen, stared out the car windows slack-jawed.

"You're kidding, right?" the kids asked. But I think they already knew the question was rhetorical.

Part I:
DISCOVERY

FALLING IN LOVE

Buyers are liars.

—Every real estate agent ever

WHEN I WAS YOUNG, my mother used to take all five of her kids on an annual quest for the family Christmas tree. We would travel around Los Angeles in our wood-paneled station wagon, from one lot of pre-cut evergreens to another, searching for the perfect tree. As the trip dragged on, there were times I questioned my mother's sanity, and yet when my mother found her tree it created a satisfaction within her that I could see even if I didn't always understand. Maybe a particular height reminded her of being a child herself; perhaps a certain shade of green reached into her soul. I never really knew, and perhaps knowing was never the point. When I would ask what she was looking for, my mother would just smile and say: "It has to talk to me."

Any honest real estate agent will tell you that most home buyers' decisions are no more rational than my mother's with her tree. There was a time in my life, years after I first encountered that ramshackle house in Port Townsend, when I was an agent myself, walking buyers through the process and dutifully helping them draw up their lists of requirements. I would listen to a couple emphatically assert that they needed four bedrooms, two baths, and a no-maintenance yard—and then watch as they fell in love with a tiny garden-becalmed cottage that they spotted on the way to the house that met every one of their specifications. It happened over and over and over. While we might like to believe that our house needs are pragmatic line items, our true needs, the ones that drive our decisions, come far more often from some deep and unacknowledged wellspring of memories and desires.

Because here's the thing—we aren't looking for a house; we're looking for a home. A house can supply you with a place to sleep, to cook, to store your car. A home fits your soul. In ancient Rome, the term *domus*, from which we get the word *domicile*, meant both *people* and *place*, an unspoken relationship that we feel like a heartbeat. A home fulfills needs you didn't know you had, so it is no wonder that when pressed for an explanation for our choices we give reasons that make no sense, pointing to a bunch of dried lavender hanging in the kitchen, a porch swing, the blue of a front door—almost always things that could be re-created in a house that fits the list. But sense is not the point. These small details are simply visual indicators of an architectural personality that fits our own, that reminds us of a childhood home, or a house, filled with color and the laughter of children, that we visited on a vacation in Mexico.

And yet a choice of a home is not just about where we've been or what we remember; it's also about who we want to be. As Winston Churchill famously said: "We shape our buildings and afterwards they shape us." When we choose a house, we are making a decision about how we will live. I don't mean in the obvious way of how long your commute to work will be, or whether there are schools or stores or friends nearby—although all of those things are important and will impact your life. What I am talking about is something far more subliminal. The designs of our homes quite literally change us. An eating nook for two invites a busy couple to slow down every morning for coffee. A courtyard in an apartment building helps create community. A south-facing window encourages optimism, while alcoves foster book lovers. Perhaps one of the strongest blows for feminism came from the first sledgehammer that opened a kitchen to a family room and changed the view of the cook, from both sides of the wall.

It is the rare buyer who sees these things for what they are. We are understandably distracted by the stress of what is for many of us the biggest financial decision of our lives. Our minds are busy. But we feel those subtle calls. We see that bunch of lavender. And as often as not, we leap.

THEY ARE GLORIOUS THINGS, these leaps into love. We catch the wind of our own enthusiasm, and off we go, into the sky of a new future. But are they really as untethered as they seem? In his book *Blink*, Malcolm Gladwell talks about our instantaneous decisions—flashes of insight he says are messages from the adaptive unconscious, the part of the brain that sifts through the bits and pieces of what is before us, focusing in on what is truly important. The process, Gladwell assures us, is a rational one; it simply "moves a little faster and operates a little more mysteriously than the kind of deliberate, conscious decision making that we usually associate with 'thinking.'" We meet a stranger and experience an instant aversion or affection. We walk in a front door for the first time and feel at home.

It's not just our minds that make these decisions, however. We live in bodies with five senses, and the stimuli they receive from our external environments have a far greater effect upon our thinking than we know. It doesn't take much to tip our decision-making scales, either. In one study, something as simple as the weight of a clipboard affected subjects' opinions of the professionalism and intellect of the otherwise equally qualified candidates they were interviewing. The heavier the board in the subjects' hands, the more likely they would be to hire the candidate. Our physical senses are busy little puppeteers, playing with the strings of our emotions. So watch out for the pleasurable feel beneath your fingers of that smooth door handle, the satisfying click of the latch as it closes tight and secure. From such seemingly innocuous interactions are big decisions made.

It can be hard to accept that our choices are being swayed by our senses, or that there is a hidden part of our brain that knows our needs better than we do ourselves. And yet what would be wrong with a moment of unconscious communication between house and human—the kind that allows for that back-of-the-mind sorting of memories and desires, along with the equally unspoken delight our senses take in a curving front path or a kitchen that smells like home? It is the totality of each of us that will live in the house, after all.

And thus, if we leap, perhaps it is with a greater safety net than we thought—flying toward a house that calls us by a name we have long forgotten, or simply need to grow into.

STUDIES–AND NOVELS AND POETRY, and general common sense— tell us that we are inclined to make leaps into love during periods of transition. One is more often propelled to jump when the ground is already shaking beneath one's feet. My husband's and my desire for a dilapidated house fit that behavior pattern rather too well.

When we found the house in Port Townsend, our family of four had recently returned to Seattle after a two-year relocation to Bergamo, Italy. Living in Bergamo had been a form of time travel. The kids were seven and ten years old when we landed in the small walled town, a fairy tale of cobblestones and bell towers. Stone buildings hugged the narrow, winding streets, and as we walked among them we inhaled the smell of slow-cooking sauces coming from homes that families had owned for generations. Stores were closed on Sundays, when families gathered together. Every once in a while, we were invited to a Sunday lunch, afternoons that turned into evenings while conversation and time unfurled.

We'd come from a world of high-tech start-ups, of dinners made from boxes and often eaten without Ben, who worked late. We believed in independence and self-sufficiency, in changing things we did not like, the sooner, the better. We'd lived light on our feet, thousands of miles away from either of our extended families. We had chosen that life every step of the way. We loved the speed and efficiency of it. We were impressed at how much you could get done.

During those two years in Italy, however, we changed. We slowed, looked around. And I realized that, more than anything else, I wanted the roots I saw in the people who surrounded us, the kind that settled deep into your heart.

But I'd learned, too, that we could never have them there. The people I met in Bergamo inhabited their town with a seamlessness that was breathtaking. They were its geography, its topography. There was no chance that we Americans, living there for only a short time, could ever put down roots among their ancient cobblestones.

So when the US company Ben worked for shut down its Bergamo office and sent us home, my feelings were mixed. That Italian way of life had sunk into us. We'd learned how to breathe air rich with tradition. On the other hand, I knew our only hope to get the kind of roots we wanted was, ironically, to leave, to go back to Seattle where we had a house and friends. It was a risky proposition, however.

"How long before we revert?" I asked Ben as we sat on the plane heading home. How long before we lost the delicious slowness of unencumbered Sundays?

"Six months?" he guessed.

It had taken two.

IN BERGAMO, WE HAD lived in a small sun-drenched apartment where the ten-foot-tall windows of the living room functioned like a magnet for humans. In that bright, open room, there was always a jigsaw puzzle in the process of completion; homework and language lessons were done there, as well, at the same table where we ate our meals. The space was an invitation to gather, a domestic equivalent of the piazza that lay in the center of the old town. Life happened there.

Whether it was that living room, or the fact that Ben was home for dinner every night, I couldn't say—but during that time we became a family in a way we'd never been before. We'd always loved each other, but it had been as a team facing the world together, looking out. As we lingered in that room, we looked toward each other, and the difference was marked.

We'd returned to Seattle—to busy lives and our Craftsman bungalow with its labyrinthine layout and a north-facing living room that sunlight never reached. I watched as our family broke into individuals who raced off to bedrooms and offices, and I missed not just the country we had left behind but, even more importantly, who we had been there. I looked longingly at real estate listings on the pastoral islands that dotted nearby Puget Sound. I envisioned a life lived slower, a house that would bring us together again.

"I want to sell the house," I told Ben.

"But we just moved home," he said.

There is a difference between logic and knowledge sometimes, and it defies articulation. I whirled in that house, unable to explain what I felt.

I tried making changes. I got the fireplace working again in the living room to add warmth and light to its dark space. I cooked all the time—pasta sauces, cookies—using smells to lure my children into the kitchen, the one truly communal part of our house. When my daughter, a newly minted American teenager, would call after school saying she wouldn't be home for dinner, I learned to pause.

"That's too bad," I'd say, letting the words drift toward her. "I cooked."

"What'd you make?" she'd ask. I could almost feel the hook catch.

And she would come home, often with friends. But it wasn't enough. I could feel us slipping from each other, losing our centers. Ben's working hours were lengthening again, while Kate's role models seemed limited solely to Britney Spears. Ten-year-old Ry was having a hard time reacculturating, boiling pasta every morning and packing it in a Tupperware container for his school lunch. I felt lost, back in a country where stay-at-home mothering was viewed less as a choice than an inability to do anything else—and I was failing even at that. I would walk through the deserted living room, up the stairs, and past my children's closed bedroom doors, and the restlessness would begin again.

"How about we look for a piece of land?" Ben suggested one day, in the spirit of diversion and compromise. "Something we can build on later, after the kids are gone?" And that was how it started.

LIKE MOST PIONEERS IN search of cheap acreage, we headed west. In our case, that meant toward the Olympic Peninsula, a huge swath of land on the far side of Puget Sound, a place with more trees than people. We spent Sundays driving from peaks to valleys, but we always seemed to end up in Port Townsend, a small Victorian seaport that clings to the northeast corner of the peninsula like some exquisite limpet. We said we went there because we were rewarding our children's patience with pizza, but there was something about the rhythm of that town. We walked among the century-old brick buildings of its waterfront, and time slowed to a speed we'd been in danger of forgetting. Gradually, the plan for land changed into the vision of a small and inexpensive cottage in town that we could rent out, covering our costs until the time when Ben and I could retire there. Something turnkey, simple, easy. A smart investment.

"Let's just drive around," Ben said.

And that, of course, is how we ended up with a four-bedroom wreck of a house.

"BUT WHY *THAT* HOUSE?" my mother asked me—a question I found amusing, coming from Our Lady of the Christmas Tree. But my mother had good reason to be skeptical. Among the five kids in our family, my role had always been "the cautious one." In addition, while we'd lived in four different houses while I was growing up, none of them had been more than twenty-five years old, and there hadn't been much need for remodeling. So while Ben and I had made some changes to our Seattle home, there wasn't much reason to think that I would want to take on, let alone be successful at, the complete renovation of a ninety-two-year-old house crammed with trash.

What I find to be the loveliest bit of irony, though, is that the seeds of the desire to save the house in Port Townsend were actually planted by my mother, long before I even knew what a mortgage was. My mother loved books and always made sure we had plenty of them. As a young child, perhaps my favorite was Virginia Lee Burton's *The Little House*. It tells the story of a small pastoral cottage that is slowly but surely surrounded by the city, growing more and more decrepit and forgotten until finally someone finds it, picks it up, and moves it out to the country again. Each time my mother read the book to me, I could feel the house's happiness, then sadness, then joy. I wanted to live in its glowing early iteration. When the city came in and the house despaired, all I wanted to do was save it.

I THINK ANYONE WHO saves an old house has to be a caretaker at heart, a believer in underdogs, someone whose imagination is inspired by limitations, not endless options. When I was a real estate agent, I used to ask my clients how they cooked. They usually thought I was trying to find out what kind of kitchen they wanted—and that was true, in part. But the question was really a way to find out how they approached life. Those who had little interest in cooking generally had even less in home maintenance and remodeling. Chefs who loved the planning of a meal—from researching recipes to finding the right ingredients—often had the temperament to design their own homes, and they could envision stunning remodels. But a fixer-upper requires a different kind of creativity, the kind that you often find in a cook whose mind is awakened by opening a refrigerator to an odd assortment of ingredients, knowing that dinner must come out of it. A cook sees leftovers as a chance to make something new and beautiful, and when someone with this kind of personality sees an old house, they are likely to want to save it. *Save* being the operative word, because for this group, the relationship with the house will be extremely personal and interactive.

I am a cook, a champion of underdogs—not just leftover ingredients, but long-forgotten novelists, stray pets, and, especially, houses. My children learned early on to divert my attention any time we passed a falling-down barn, or a house with good bones and paint that was peeling like a third-degree sunburn.

"Mom's going to want that one," Ry would say, shaking his head.

"It needs us," I'd answer. But in the past, I'd never done anything about it. We'd driven on, and I'd held those enchanting wrecks in my mind, and at night when I couldn't sleep I would mull over the possibilities of how I could save them, the same way other people count sheep.

BUT WHY WAS IT *that* house, out of all the ones I'd seen over the years? Did I see symmetry and balance in its shape? Did I see a project, an outlet for a frustrated mind? Was it the big, wide porch underneath that rampant camellia, a vision of a time when people used to sit in rocking chairs and call out to their neighbors as they passed? Or was the house just the equivalent of picking up a lost puppy, on a very large scale?

I couldn't have told you then. At the time, the back of my mind was doing the thinking, efficiently spinning through all the intricacies of the decision and finding the real reasons underneath. Maybe it knew better than I that I wasn't ready to acknowledge the lessons I needed to learn, the ones the house could teach me. So among all the details, it grasped on to the delicate, undulating curves of a corbel, an unnecessary architectural flourish tucked in the corner where the front porch pillar met the roof, far above the trash, and handed that image to my conscious self. Said: *Here you go. This is what you want.*

A moment of beauty. A glimpse of a slower life in the midst of chaos.

IT HAS BEEN MANY years now since that day. During that time, the house has been just what the corbel promised. It has also been the exact opposite. But in the end, the back of my mind was right—this was the house I needed. I just didn't understand why yet.

SPIRIT OF PLACE

We had come without knowing it
to our inevitable place.
—Robinson Jeffers

IT HAD BEEN OUR real estate agent's idea that Ben and I drive around on our own and find houses we were attracted to, so that she could get a better idea of what we wanted. This was obviously not the scenario she'd intended. But being a professional, she promised to look into it. Two days later, she called us.

"Well, you've got timing," she said. "The old man died two weeks ago." Her tone suggested that she couldn't quite decide if we were psychic or ambulance chasers.

"It's not on the market," she added, "but I can do some digging around. Are you interested?"

I thought of all the trash we'd spotted through the dusty curtains, of the discarded furnaces and the disconcerting tilt to the structure. And then I thought of the sweet back porch with its multipane windows. The river rock chimney, its lighter and darker stones arranged in whimsical patterns. Those corbels at the corner of the porch columns that had made me look up above the trash.

Possibility murmured.

Over the years since, I have learned to recognize that sound. It comes when I get the first glimmer of an image that will later turn into a book. I have learned to trust the instinct, until my conscious mind understands what my imagination is giving me. But back then, when writing a novel still seemed as inconceivable as getting that house, I could only describe the feeling as yearning.

"Yes," I said, trying to keep my voice neutral.

GIVEN THE GO-AHEAD, OUR agent suddenly displayed the skills of a crack detective, tracking down heirs and elusive estate lawyers. As it turned out, there were several of each, a cat's cradle of conflicting offspring and wills. It seemed likely the house would fall apart before there would ever be agreement among them.

"But lawyers are legally obligated to show any offers they receive to their clients," our agent told us over the phone. I could hear the thrill of the chase in her voice. "Maybe we can convince them it's better to fight over money than a house."

So we made an attention-grabbing offer, subject to inspection. To sweeten the deal, we included a provision stating that we would clean out the house if they wanted. And then we waited. And waited.

IN A TYPICAL REAL estate transaction, sellers are given twenty-four hours or so to consider a buyer's offer and make a response—but ours was no typical offer, and its window of opportunity was vast. Unwilling to lose the house simply out of impatience, we created monthlong deadlines and then renewed them over and over. Summer gave way to autumn, which lapsed into winter. At night, I would lie in bed and think of the house, uninhabited, collapsing upon itself. I would dream of water coming through that disintegrating roof, of the trash rising up and taking over, and I'd wake in the mornings with my hands clenched, tight even when I tried to open them. I began to wonder if I was getting arthritis.

Every once in a while, our real estate agent would relay messages from the lawyers: a possible warming to the idea of selling, an interest in having someone else clean out the house. We would respond positively and wait for the next indication of movement. It was like playing a fish at the end of a very long line. So intent were we upon our goal, however, that it wasn't until later that we began to wonder who was catching whom.

Sometimes, to break the tension of waiting, we would drive out to Port Townsend to make sure the house was still there. We would leave the city behind and drive winding roads through pastoral valleys that had been left behind when glaciers receded long ago. The mountains rose to our west, a towering backdrop. Each time I fell a little more in love with the quiet, open space of the Olympic Peninsula and the quirky little town at the end of our journey. Each time, it felt a little more like coming home—my own corner of a landscape I had chosen decades before.

I WAS NINETEEN THE first time I saw the Pacific Northwest, a sophomore in college traveling from Los Angeles to Seattle for a conference. The airplane banked, coming in low over an endless, intricate collage of blue and green, the mountains and bays and islands of Puget Sound curling around and into one another. My mind calmed, and it felt as if I became myself for the first time in my life.

The ancient Romans believed in something they called a *genius*, or the spirit of a thing. The protective spirit of a place was called its *genius loci*, and the Romans believed in it not as some poetic metaphor or symbol, but as a living being. Over the centuries, the meaning of the term has shifted, and the usage of genius loci has generalized to the "feel" of a place. But I like to think those spirits are still there calling to us.

And whether we pay attention to those calls or not, they influence us. We fall into some geographical settings as if they are the arms of a mother or a lover. We unconsciously prickle in the presence of others. My daughter gets hives when she leaves the city for any length of time, while my son, like my husband, relaxes into himself in the mountains. For me, that first time I saw the Pacific Northwest was like finding a geographical soul mate. When I returned "home" to Los Angeles on that trip, flying in over those miles and miles of houses splayed out in a seemingly infinite grid, I started to cry.

It wasn't until I discovered geographer Jay Appleton's theory of prospect and refuge, however, that I found a framework to explain my reaction. According to Appleton, humans are most comfortable in situations where they can observe (prospect) and feel safe (refuge) at the same time. A window seat is a classic example—enclosed and part of the house, but with a view of what is outside—an architectural re-creation of the experience of being held in a mother's arms.

When I looked through the lens of Appleton's theory, my reactions to the landscapes I have inhabited became clear. The intricate combination of the vistas and hideaways of Puget Sound is a textbook example of prospect and refuge, writ in geographical terms. Los Angeles, in contrast, is a former desert, a flat canvas painted in freeways and buildings, and when the air turns to smog and you cannot see the mountains, it can feel endless. During the years I lived there, I experienced a constant restlessness. It was hard to know who I was—not an unusual problem for me as I was growing up, but this felt different. Exterior in some way. I am the kind of person who will always take the chair in the corner, and living without geographical refuge meant that at some level I was constantly alert. I am an extreme example, certainly, but perhaps it is not all that coincidental that Los Angeles is the home of Disneyland and movies, fantasy and imagination. Sometimes the best refuge is in the mind.

IF THERE IS ONE thing that characterizes the *genius* of the Pacific Northwest, it is water. It slips down from the sky and washes up against our shores. It creates our silver-blue color palette, then softens it to pastels through the very moisture in the air. Long ago, water filled the deepest gouges left behind by those retreating glaciers, and created bays and lakes and inlets, a canal, a strait, a sound.

It is mysterious water out there in Puget Sound, an average of 450 feet deep, and unrelentingly dark. Down below resides the world's largest species of octopus—there have been reports of *Enteroctopus dofleini* as large as six hundred pounds and thirty-two feet across. Matter made fluid, their boneless bodies can squeeze through a space the size of their eyeballs; their brains circle their throats and travel down their arms. As unbelievable as Bigfoot, the giant Pacific octopi nevertheless exist, deep in the murky water, a reminder that things are still a little wild in this part of the world.

That goes double for the Olympic Peninsula, the most northern and western portion of the contiguous United States. A giant thumb of land that lies between Seattle and the Pacific Ocean, it has been isolated from rapid development by the water that flanks its three sides. As recently as 1846—when the United States gained possession of everything south of the Strait of Juan de Fuca in a border settlement with the British—there was not a single white settler on the peninsula, and even the Native Americans tended to stick to the coastline. Back then, the most numerous inhabitants were trees, evergreen behemoths over 250 feet tall, with bases 14 feet across and bark up to 12 inches thick. It's been said the sap could spurt like an oil gusher.

In his book *The Last Wilderness*, Murray Morgan wrote: "God made the universe, and when he was finished, he dumped everything left over onto the Olympic Peninsula." It is still mostly as God dumped it—3,600 square miles of mountains and rain forests dripping with moss, and a national park covering almost a million acres. The coasts are storm-smashed, with towns and the occasional Indian reservation scattered along their edges like afterthoughts.

TO MY MIND, THERE is something exciting about a place that's still a bit wild. It's probably the fault of all the Laura Ingalls Wilder books I read when I was child. Back then, I wanted to *be* Laura. One of my all-time favorite presents was a doll-sized replica of a cast-iron stove, on which I pretended to make meals for my thoroughly unimpressed Skipper and Barbie dolls. And I'm finding that the longer I live in the Pacific Northwest, the less affinity I have for the trappings of a cosmopolitan life. These days, I would rather see a well-stacked woodpile than a Broadway show, and that approach fits in just fine out here.

It's been said that geographical landscapes create their own cultural personalities. Perhaps our particular culture here in the Pacific Northwest derives from the contrast of the beautiful and the unsettling. Lying underneath all that photogenic prospect and refuge, there are earthquake faults. The shimmering water of Puget Sound is deadly cold. Mountain passes can snow shut, leaving you trapped on one side or the other, just like our pioneer ancestors. And Mount Rainier, Seattle's most beloved icon, is a sleeping volcano. Mother Nature is still in charge in this neck of the woods.

People in Seattle have a reputation for being friendly and pleasant but reserved. Perhaps it is because so many of its residents are still settling in. Or perhaps it is the knowledge—reinforced by those rugged mountains, that cold water—that you never know when you might need all your resources just to survive.

PORT TOWNSEND TAKES THAT personality and gives it a twist. Set on a peninsula where the trucks of unemployed lumberjacks display bumper stickers declaring EARTH FIRST: WE'LL LOG THE REST LATER, the town is a cultural oddity of a gently eccentric sort, its population a mildly simmering Crock-Pot of paper mill workers, artists, organic farmers, wintering Alaskan fishermen, and—more and more often these days—wealthy city runaways and retirees. One of its better-known bumper stickers sports the slogan WE'RE ALL HERE BECAUSE WE'RE NOT ALL THERE.

Port Townsend is a place that is proud of its independence. It's Washington State's per capita leader in solar power, and the vast majority of its businesses are family-owned. Deer roam freely in town (a 2016 deer census counted 238 of them), and you can sometimes hear coyotes yipping in the night. In the upper town, sidewalks are rare, and people often walk in the middle of the street, a strangely liberating activity. Port Townsend's calendar is packed with festivals, but my favorite is the kinetic-sculpture race, with its brightly colored collection of human-powered vehicles, which are more about self-expression than transportation. If this town has a *genius*, it's likely wearing a jester's hat.

It's also a place that is fiercely protective of its heritage, and with good reason. Port Townsend is a movie set waiting for cameras, one of only three architecturally preserved Victorian seaports in the United States. The waterfront is lined with two- and three-story brick buildings scarcely changed in appearance from when they were built at the end of the nineteenth century. The bluffs and hills above them are scattered with charming cottages and Queen Anne and Italianate mansions. It's a place out of time—although the reasons for that have more to do with luck, both good and bad.

"POVERTY IS THE BEST friend of preservation," Clem Labine, the founder of *Old House Journal*, has said. In the late 1880s, when most of Port Townsend's magnificent construction occurred, the dream was for a much larger city. At the time, the town was competing with Seattle to become the terminus for the railroad that was being built up the West Coast. While such a goal might seem far-fetched, looking at the two places now, back then only New York City had more marine cargo traffic than Port Townsend. Seattle, tucked far down Puget Sound, was at a distinct disadvantage when it came to trade.

The people of Port Townsend decided to take fate into their own hands, starting their own railroad heading south. Their optimism was infectious; land prices exploded, and suddenly the town of seven thousand had six banks and three streetcar systems. In 1889, the Oregon Improvement Company declared that Port Townsend would indeed be the terminus of the West Coast railroad. By the next year, however, the OIC had gone into receivership. Expansion and building in Port Townsend froze. Almost overnight, its population shrank to two thousand.

The year 1889 was a big one for Seattle as well, but its trajectory went in the opposite direction. On June 6, a woodshop worker tipped an overheated glue pot onto a pile of wood shavings, and it quickly turned into a conflagration. The tide in Puget Sound was out, the fire chief was nowhere to be found, and the commercial area of Seattle burned to the ground in hours. Afterward, a group of six hundred business owners got together and pledged to rebuild using only brick and stone. Over the next year, buildings shot up, and people flooded over the pass from the east, following the scent of possibility. By 1890, Seattle had a population of forty thousand. By 1893, it was the terminus of the Great Northern Railway.

In the years since then, many of Seattle's impressive early buildings have been demolished as the city has grown and modernized. Port Townsend, on the other hand, has remained a kind of architectural Pompeii, preserved in time by simple economics, as few residents had the money to remodel or replace those gorgeous Victorian buildings. It was 1958 before a couple from nearby Tacoma started the tradition of out-of-towners coming in and renovating. It's a catch-22, and most of the townspeople seem to know it—there isn't much local money for restoration, but it is often unclear whether the newcomers will value the history of the houses enough to preserve them.

IT WAS AN ATTITUDE that Ben and I understood. When we first moved to Seattle in 1982, the city was still reeling from the massive Boeing layoffs of the 1970s, and the software industry was barely in its beginning stages. It hadn't been that long since there'd been a billboard up in the city that read WILL THE LAST PERSON LEAVING SEATTLE - TURN OUT THE LIGHTS. But after the hustle of Los Angeles, Seattle was a paradise to us. Ben and I were grad-student poor, and while we looked for an apartment that first August, we ate our lunches off the blackberry bushes that covered the city like generosity itself. At school, the other teaching assistants looked at me strangely when I automatically flicked my keys between my fingers for safety as I left the English department building in the evening. There was no need for that here, they explained.

But that changed over the decades we lived there. It is estimated that Microsoft alone created twelve thousand millionaire employees, and all that money shifted things. Other technology companies rushed in. Lured by jobs or the natural setting, people came from all across the country. The city turned into something brighter, sharper, and certainly more congested. Ben and I knew we were part of the problem; we were transplants ourselves, and software was how Ben ended up making a living. But that didn't stop us from mourning the changes in our city and contemplating a change for ourselves.

And so now here we were, part of the latest wave of newcomers splashing up on the shores of Port Townsend. Our purpose was to save a house that was already there, but why should the locals trust us? Who was to say we wouldn't just grab the land and do whatever we wanted?

Ben and I couldn't fault the local wariness; it is natural to want to protect what you love. It was how we felt about the house, after all. But as we waited for a response from the heirs—one month after another after another—I told myself that perhaps in the end it wouldn't matter what the locals thought. If the heirs didn't make a decision sometime soon, there would be no house left to save.

MAINTENANCE

A peculiar kind of maniac who is one part
ability, one part inventiveness, two parts
determination, three parts romanticism,
and six parts damn foolishness.

—George Nash, describing "old-house people"

FINALLY, AFTER MORE THAN half a year, we got the call.

"It's yours!" our agent exclaimed. And with that, we were vaulted into a ten-day inspection period. Technically, the control in the situation had been handed to us, but it felt more like that moment after too long standing, shivering, at the top of a ski run, when someone simply pushes you from behind and you start flying down the slope.

"I know a great inspector," our agent said.

"Will you be there?" I asked.

"I have another appointment," she said quickly, although we hadn't yet set a date.

IN A NORMAL SITUATION, ten days is plenty of time to go through a house with an experienced inspector, even to have an old sewer line scoped or to bring in an engineer if things look questionable. Generally, however, the buyers have spent a fair amount of time in the house already. Because our house had never gone on the market, the inspection would be our first opportunity to go inside. They say love is blind; in our case it was almost literally true.

On a cold, clear January morning, we arrived at the house to find a truck from the Port Townsend water department and a visibly agitated man standing next to it.

"Is this your place?" he asked, approaching us with a wrench held loosely in his hand. I took a step back.

"No. I mean, not yet. We're just doing an inspection," Ben said in as friendly a tone as he could muster.

"Well, you've got problems," the man said. "When I tried to turn on the water, I got shocked clear back into the street. Just about fried my brain cells."

As he marched off, another truck arrived—Ron, the inspector. Ron was a lanky man with short white hair and a big smile that showed off the gold braces on his teeth. He looked up at the house, and I saw an expression of admiration flash across his face.

"You know, I've watched this one for a long time," he said. "They don't make 'em like this anymore." Then he whipped out a respirator from the front seat of his truck.

"I do this in every house," he said reassuringly.

I didn't believe him for a second.

"Ready?" he asked.

"Sure," Ben replied, and he and I nervously followed Ron toward the front steps.

IN THE EMOTIONALLY TUMULTUOUS process of buying a house, an inspector provides a bulwark of sanity. It is his job (and it is almost universally a "he") to see the things we home buyers don't. While we float along in the land of fantasy, imagining how we'll fill the rooms, an inspector is dealing with more concrete matters, as it were. In his book *Renovating Old Houses*, George Nash suggests a checklist for a house inspection that is a staggering thirty-two items long. The list includes, in order of decreasing importance and expense, everything from structural timbers to electrical systems, exterior trim paint, and bathroom fixtures. At the very bottom comes one last item: "Does it feel right?"

Unless you are a house geek—or very brave—an inspection is often the lowest point in the buying process. Real estate agents gear up for it, knowing their clients will have a dip in enthusiasm that can slide into an extreme depression. As potential home buyers, we fall for a dream and then are forced to deal with the reality of things that we may not know how, or cannot afford, to fix. Even an inspection of the cleanest house can have this effect—we don't like someone taking potshots at our new love. But a good inspector will give you both clarity and solutions, and then let you make up your own mind. It's not fun, but it's a critical point in the process, and paying attention can help avoid much heartache later.

George Nash says, in *Renovating Old Houses,* that it's "commonplace that a marriage needs more than the first flush of passion to sustain itself. Likewise, even if it's love at first sight, you shouldn't buy an old house without conducting a thorough investigation into even its most uninviting corners." His comparison of marriage to house inspections has always made me wonder how many weddings would go forward if couples went through a similar process before the big day, complete with a checklist of current and potential future defects. Foundation—rotten, or not. Electricity—inadequate for the load, or with plenty to spare. That sheltering roof—watertight, or with leaks.

Back in the first century BC, the Roman engineer Vitruvius had a simpler method of determining a good building, which architects still follow today. Vitruvius was creating buildings from scratch, but his principles apply equally well for house inspections. He wrote that to be an example of good architecture, a building must have *firmitas, utilitas,* and *venustas.* These Latin words have been translated in different ways, but I like this version best: stability, utility, and beauty. Would that we could all have those traits.

AS RON, BEN, AND I forged our way up onto the front porch, I could only hope that our house might display some of Vitruvius's principles—or at least get a passing mark on any of the items from Nash's checklist. To get to the door, we threaded cautiously between busted bags of potting soil, knocking a hip against an old motorcycle, a shin on a rusted pesticide sprayer. Through the greying weave of the curtains, we could see a dense jungle of shapes inside.

When we finally reached the front door, we encountered a brand-new lockset, bright against the dirty white paint. It was the first and only sign of home maintenance we had seen. There were several possible reasons for it, but I realized that it was unlikely I could ever accurately guess which one, or even who had done it.

Ben and I looked at each other. "Is it keeping people out, or stuff in?" he asked.

The key turned with a simple click, but the door resisted our polite and then increasingly forthright pressure against it. The ancient Romans said even doors have a spirit. This one seemed to be warning us—or snarling. I couldn't tell which. I put my hand against the worn paint of the doorframe and felt it peeling beneath my touch.

"Let us in," I said under my breath.

ONE OF MY CARDINAL rules when I was a real estate agent was: Wear nice socks. It's a corollary to the classic maternal admonition never to wear torn underwear, in case you're in an accident and have to be taken to the hospital. Real estate agents are constantly touring homes and are often faced with the choice of taking off their shoes or putting on the dreaded blue paper booties, which make even the most stylish agent look like an incompetent surgeon. But that was not my reason for choosing the former option, because I will always take off my shoes, whether required to or not, and I encouraged my clients to do the same.

Without shoes, we pay more attention to our sensory interactions with a building. One of my favorite examples of this is the message inherent in the worn indentations in old stone stairs. You can almost feel the river of people who traveled before you, smoothing that stone like water. There is history in every step you take, and you become part of it as you add your own moments of friction, foot against stone. Your individual contribution matters, and yet the stone of the steps would not change, soften, without all those other feet that have—and will—travel across them. Imagine those same stairs replaced with functional grated metal, and history disappears.

As we move through a building, our bodies—hardwired to scan our surroundings for danger, joy, sustenance—are tracking every-thing, sending us messages through our senses. By eliminating my shoes, I bring myself closer in contact with a house. Without the dis-traction of heels, I have learned to sense the slope of a floor, noting the times when my balance seems slightly off-kilter. I can feel if the owner has skimped on the pad for that new carpet laid just before putting the house on the market—and if so, I look for other signs of quick fixes in more crucial areas. I watch out for the slight headache that can arrive in a basement, a sure sign my nose has picked up an odor of mold too faint for my conscious mind. If I enter a house that has those plug-in fragrance emitters, I disconnect them if possible. Perhaps the owners have been told a synthetic scent will sell their house—or perhaps they are covering up years of cigarette smoke or pets. In any case, they have placed a barrier between me and their house, and my mind, set off by my nose, reacts with an unconscious distancing that can color the rest of the tour.

These small physical reactions can work in the other direction, too, pushing our emotions ahead of rational thought. The old trick of baking an apple pie before an open house is a classic because it works. So, too, do warm tiles underfoot, smooth paint on a banister, or the dreamy waves in old window glass. One of my favorite things about our apartment in Italy was the antique key we were given for the front gate. I relished the weight of it in my hand, the angular notches in the bit, the clunking sound it made as it turned and opened those massive wrought-metal gates. I still have that key, stolen as we moved out because I couldn't bear to part with it.

THERE WOULD BE NO taking off of shoes in the house in Port Townsend. By the time we finally got the front door open, using a full-shoulder shove, it was already obvious there was a problem with the foundation. Nothing but a bad foundation can make a door stick in one corner like that. I didn't need bare feet to tell me—and I would definitely need my shoes for the rest of the journey. If I'd had any illusions otherwise, the question was laid to rest as the light from the open door hit the living room. This was a house for hip boots.

The piles appeared first. Five-foot-tall towers of boxes spread in a slowly disintegrating sprawl across the room, spilling old photos, hammers, pink Bibles, and patent leather shoes, like birdseed from a split bag. A wide soot-covered fireplace dominated the south wall, a black woodstove thrusting out from the hearth like a squat, angry badger. Beside it resided a television the size of a small refrigerator; next to it were two more televisions, each one about twelve years older than the last. Their boxes stood nearby. A footpath led through the stacks to the dining room, revealing a glimpse of dirty red carpet.

I yanked my sleeves over my hands. It was cold anyway, January inside as well as out, which was probably what was keeping the smell to a manageable level. Ron's respirator was starting to seem smarter by the minute. I pulled my turtleneck up over my nose and followed the sound of underwater breathing into the next room.

If the living room had been full, the dining room was packed, a carnival fun house of objects. Black metal shelving units covered the walls, crammed with dead plants in pink plastic pots, faded boxes of baking soda and cough medicine, a wooden model ferryboat, a fishing rod, cheese graters, and meat grinders. A huge yellowed bra lolled out of a drawer in an overstuffed sideboard, next to a miniature ceramic Saint Bernard, and a neon-painted tourist plate depicting the wonders of Seattle's Space Needle. Scanning the room, my eye caught on a faded doctor's invoice for a pregnancy test, dropped casually on top of one of the stacks of papers that covered the table in an unruly skyline.

I looked at it, confused. We hadn't wanted to know much about the previous owner—ironic, considering we had offered to dispose of his personal possessions—but the one thing I did know was that he had been a widower, his children grown and gone.

I looked around the room again. I'd never been anywhere like this before. My childhood home had been neater and more organized than I was comfortable with—an opinion I'd stated regularly as I moved into my own house, had children, and let their laundry collect on the bathroom floor for a day or two. I wanted a more relaxed life, I'd said, asserting my independence.

But whatever that was in the dining room of the house in Port Townsend, it wasn't relaxed. It felt alive, vibrating, hungry. I turned toward Ben. In the past, we had made a game of walking through open houses and making up stories about the people who lived there, playing detective in a casual kind of way. But this was different, disquieting, like a stranger's eyes meeting yours right before the bus hits.

"Let's see the view," Ben said, muscling his way over to the window. As he pulled back the heavy curtains, the outside flowed in— Victorian rooftops, the tips of trees, the water beyond. I breathed in slowly through my turtleneck, inhaling the smell of my own skin.

"Now that's a nice view," Ron said. "Remember that."

He walked over to the swinging door on the west wall of the dining room. It seemed likely it would lead to the narrow room that extended out from that side of the house—a butler's pantry had been our best guess when we'd viewed it from the outside. Ron pushed open the door, and I caught a glimpse of a stove with something ancient and orange dripping down its dull white front, towers of dishes in a grey-tinged sink, a sagging ceiling, and green indoor-outdoor carpet, curling like waves at the edges. The kitchen, if you could call it that.

"Okay then," Ron said, closing the door firmly and heading toward the staircase to the second floor.

In my mind, I had already started checking off items. *Firmitas* was a definite no. And according to the expression on the inspector's face, *utilitas* was falling by the wayside as well. When I raised my eyebrows in question to him, he just said, "Water," shaking his head.

"THE ROOT OF ALL EVIL is water," writes Stewart Brand, the author of *How Buildings Learn.* "It consumes wood, erodes masonry, corrodes metals, peels paint, expands destructively when it freezes, and permeates everywhere when it evaporates." And it takes remarkably little for water to gain access to a building and begin its work. You don't need a hurricane or a flood. All it takes is a missing roof shingle. Peeling paint. A crack in a window frame. In the end, Ben and I would learn that the vast majority of our structural problems could be traced back to a single downspout that had fallen off and never been replaced. One. Single. Downspout.

WHEN YOU STEP BACK and look at the issue from a larger perspective, we really shouldn't be surprised when our buildings succumb to the treachery of nature. In most parts of the United States, houses are made of wood—or, to put it another way, dead trees. Nature has its own plan for dead trees: When one falls, water, dirt, and insects move in to begin the labor of decomposition. It can take a long time—for the grandest of Douglas firs, it may require hundreds of years—but decomposition always prevails.

We humans interrupt the cycle. We take the tree while it's still alive, remove its protective bark, and, from its most vulnerable parts, create our homes. From that point on, preservation depends almost entirely on keeping out the elements of nature—even though rain, dirt, and insects virtually surround the house, and the wood is easily the most exposed part. Seen in this light, concrete foundations, solid roofs, unblemished coats of paint, and tight-fitting windows are all merely stopgap attempts to keep nature from following a system whose efficacy was proven millennia ago. It doesn't take much thinking before the whole thing begins to seem a little foolhardy.

The early Pacific Northwest settlers built out of wood for a simple reason: that's what was here. Creating space for a farm, a town, or a store meant clearing trees, their stumps, and their god-awful roots. And while certainly there were stones in the ground, it only made sense to use timber for building. Those early forests are mostly gone, but lumber remains the cheapest and most plentiful building product available.

Wood is how many new cultures begin, until the land is cleared, the trees are chopped, and all that is left is rocks. When we get down to stones, houses gain a shot at permanency; human history defies fire and water and bugs, grabs on to the land, and holds. We get Colosseums and Buckingham Palaces, whitewashed Irish cottages next to dry-stacked rock walls. The shift from wood to stone construction in northern Europe was considered to be of such importance it was given a name: "The Great Rebuilding" in England; "The Victory of Stone over Wood" in France. Slogans for a new era.

For those of us in the United States, and particularly the Northwest, our timber houses are perhaps our most potent daily reminder that we are still a young society, not yet out of the woods. Our houses cannot last forever, their life expectancy centuries less than one of those big Douglas firs lying unprotected on the ground, or their stone counterparts in Europe. Suddenly, that old children's story about the three little pigs takes on a whole new meaning.

THE PROBLEM IS, FEW people are invigorated by the idea of spending their precious Sundays caulking the trim of their windows or getting up on their roofs to check for moss. As Brand puts it: "The romance of maintenance is that it has none." Even back in 1994, it was estimated that only a third of US houses were actually well maintained, and it was predicted that number would drop as people's work hours increased— as they have. And when people aren't watching out, water, rodents, termites, and mold move in. It makes sense; we've logged much of the forests that were their natural habitat. They're only looking for a substitute home, and negligence on our part just makes their hunt easier.

The act of maintenance, however, can have its own particular beauty. "There is a certain higher calling in the steady tending to a ship, to a garden, to a building," Brand writes. "One is participating physically in a deep, long life." Perhaps my favorite example of this approach to maintenance can be found in the story of the dining hall at New College, Oxford, which was established in the fourteenth century. The dining hall is a stunning room, with high, beamed ceilings built from massive oak trees, like a set from a Harry Potter movie. Over time, however, oak beams become infested with beetles. It's a known fact, and there is little that could have been done about it, particularly back in those centuries before we had access to so many chemicals. In any case, about a hundred years ago, it was discovered that the beams had become "beetly." The problem was that there were few oaks anymore that were big enough to use for beams—especially in England, where most of the trees had been cut down centuries before.

But someone thought to ask the college forester (I love that there is such a position), in the hope that there might be some big oaks hanging around that would work. The forester came in and, as anthropologist Gregory Bateson told the story, he said, "Well, sirs, we was wonderin' when you'd be askin'."

It turned out that when the college was founded, a grove of oaks was planted to provide the replacements for the beams they knew would fall victim to beetles by the time the new trees matured. For five hundred years, the message had been relayed from one generation of foresters to the next: "You don't cut them oaks. Them's for the College Hall."

It's a wonderful story, and I try to think about it when I am grumbling about repainting my peeling front porch steps or repairing the grout between the bathroom tiles. For things to last, we must think long-term.

IN AN ODD WAY, marriages deal with many of the same maintenance issues. Our relationships need our attention as much, if not more, than our houses. And sometimes here, too, the romance of maintenance is that it has none. Caretaking in a relationship is not flowers or date night—necessary as these are, they are the equivalent of a new color painted on your walls. Delightful, but not structural. Structural is unloading the dishwasher when it's your partner's turn, or making sure whoever gets home last from work is greeted with dinner. It's learning about mushroom hunting or musical theater or rugby because your spouse loves it. It is talking about the best of your partner in public, not the worst. It's listening to stories we have heard a hundred times before as if they are new. Often, it is just listening, period.

My father always washed the car by hand before he took my mother out on a date, even after they were married. He would say he wanted it clean "for his girl." That is the part she remembered, not where they went or what they did. As psychologist John Gottman, who has studied countless married couples, will tell you, it is the presence of respect and an abiding willingness to support each other, more than romance, that indicates whether a marriage will last. Couples that exhibit these qualities tend to stay together, creating the marital equivalent of *firmitas*.

As I followed Ben up the stairs in the Port Townsend house, I was hoping we were doing well in the marriage department, but I worried sometimes that we threw ourselves at things like this because the excitement of a questionable project seemed more romantic, or at the very least more dramatic, than the caretaking of a relationship. It is perhaps why many marriages founder during a remodel or a building project—it isn't really about needing a new kitchen or house. Sensing a lack in their relationship, some couples rush toward a project or a baby when in fact those voids might be better filled by words spoken to each other. By simple maintenance, instead of a new addition.

The jury was still out on where Ben and I fell on that spectrum. The truth is, though, that many of the things I love best about Ben come out during our crazy projects—his gift of envisioning what isn't there, his reliable sense of humor, his artistic sensibilities, not to mention his MacGyver-like abilities. On one of our first dates, a trip into the Los Angeles mountains, he fixed my car's leaking gas line by rechewing an old piece of gum he'd found in the ashtray and plugging the hole until we could get to a gas station. The fact that I found this immensely appealing says much about us.

In many ways, Ben and I are at our best in challenging situations. Over the course of our relationship, we'd moved far away from family, and left good, practical jobs to chase dreams. We'd had children when we were without any foreseeable income. We'd even adopted a puppy, sight unseen, when our son was three months old and our daughter a toddler. That the last one had seemed the craziest of all to us tells you something.

Maybe—probably—I worry too much, I told myself. So I crossed my fingers and headed upstairs.

THE CHAOS WE'D ENCOUNTERED on the main floor extended to the second. A claw-foot bathtub sat in the middle of the first bedroom, filled to overflowing with what looked like forty years of clothes and board games and sports equipment. We tried to enter the other bedrooms, but the doors would open only enough for a peek inside. Peering in through the crack of a door, I saw more piles of clothes, a camping porta-potty, a rifle.

"Oh, man," I heard Ron say, backing out of the bathroom, his voice muffled by the respirator.

"E, come here," Ben called to me. "You've got to see this." He pointed to the shower.

It was the soap I saw first—a delicate sculpture made up of some fifty slivers of Irish Spring, thin as porcelain. A precarious tower of green and white rising up in the back corner. More work to stack them than to throw them away, and yet there they were, balancing.

"The faucet." Ben redirected my attention.

I looked and then looked again, puzzled. The handles were covered with yellow rubber kitchen gloves secured with rubber bands. They looked like Mickey Mouse hands, waving at me from the tile wall. But that didn't make sense. I turned to Ben.

"So he wouldn't get electrocuted," he remarked dryly.

That would explain what had happened to the guy from the water company: the plumbing was live.

There were a couple potential explanations for this situation. A rat could have chewed away the insulation of a wire that then came to rest on a pipe. Or—and we were beginning to think this was more likely—someone had grounded a live wire instead of a neutral one to a pipe, as would normally happen. In any case, whoever was taking showers had preferred to risk death rather than fix the problem. It was kind of impressive when you thought about it.

Except there was already too much to think about. Of the thirty-plus items on Nash's checklist, the best we could hope for was a neutral ranking on a few. The only thing that would garner full praise in this house was the view—and that didn't require the house.

The rule of thumb is that if the renovation will cost more than half the purchase price, you should just start over. It was already clear that we would need to renegotiate with the heirs based on what we'd found, but even then, it was obvious that fixing this house would likely cost more than we would pay to buy it.

Ben and I shared a look: *Do you still want it?* He wasn't saying no.

Send me something, I said to the house in my mind. *Give me a reason.* Because strangely enough, I still wanted one.

RON HAD FOUND AN entrance to the attic. When it was my turn, Ben held the ladder and I climbed up the rungs, expecting the worst. But as the beam from the flashlight roved over the darkened space, I could see the straight lines of rafters, the untouched interior of a roof soaring above me. Everything felt quiet, peaceful, as if this one portion of the house had somehow kept itself separate from all that had happened below—as if in some way, it was only itself. For the first time, I felt the house as it had once been.

THE ARCHITECT JACQUES HERZOG has suggested an interesting take on Vitruvius's three principles of *firmitas, utilitas,* and *venustas*. He posits that certain buildings are so strong and utilitarian that they generate instability through their very lack of beauty. Take, for example, Pruitt-Igoe, the high-rise public housing project built in 1954 as a solution to the lack of low-income housing in Saint Louis and demolished after only eighteen years. The lack of shared green space and the unrelieved repetition of nearly identical floors and hallways, reached only by elevators or isolated stairwells, which rapidly became the domain of drug dealers—all of that killed any sense of community and led to graffiti, crime, and a general hatred of the place. The structure did not fail in any technical sense, but its excessive utility at the expense of beauty created its demise.

On the flip side of this equation are the gardens and temples of the city of Kyoto, Japan. They are built from far more fragile materials, but they contain a beauty that inspires people to maintain them. In fact, some historians contend that the city of Kyoto was spared in the bombing of Japan during World War II because US Secretary of War Henry L. Stimson had spent his honeymoon there and couldn't stand the thought of such a lovely place being destroyed. Beauty created its own durability.

SO THERE I STOOD, toes holding on to the rung of a ladder. I leaned forward into the still, perfect space of the attic, and in that moment all the defects of the house mattered not at all. I went for the last item on Nash's list: *Does it feel right?*

"It's okay," I whispered into the dark. "It's not your fault. We'll take care of you."

THE FOUR Rs

*A remodeler's tool of choice is
invariably the wrecking bar.*
—George Nash

AND SO WE PUT ON OUR hard hats and renegotiated. We showed the heirs the horrifying inspection report, trying to get to a price that made any of this possible. All we really learned is that owners are rarely rational about their houses. Following the heirs' line of thinking, if the house had not fallen while they lived there, it never would.

It took weeks, but we finally reached a compromise that made no one exactly happy but allowed ownership to change hands. The house would be ours. Now we just had to figure out what to do with it.

EVER SINCE WORD HAD gotten around town that we were trying to buy the house, people had started questioning us.

"Would you be remodeling?"

"Restoring?"

"Renovating?"

To which we'd consistently and proudly answered yes—as in, yes, we wanted to keep the house, not tear it down. But we came to understand that these three terms meant vastly different things. I'd never heard the distinction in Seattle, where the population is numerous and ever changing, and landmark buildings are too often destroyed in the name of progress. But Port Townsend was different, and people there cared what happened to their buildings. And it wasn't just the houses, either.

"You gonna keep those palm trees?" an old man asked as he walked by.

I looked at the trees—two mangy four-foot-tall specimens, kidnapping victims from a sunnier climate, their fronds drooping despondently toward the ground as if they hoped it might be warmer there. It made me cold just to look at them.

"They're how people navigate around here," the old man said. "Turn right at the palm trees." He gave me a considering look. "I'd hate to have to write a letter to the newspaper," he finished, pleasantly enough.

I wondered what he would think if he knew we were thinking about cutting the kitchen off the side of the house.

HOME REMODELING AND MAINTENANCE in the United States was a 320-billion-dollar business in 2016, and the number is expected only to rise. But for most people entering this fray, there is little discussion of the distinction between the three *R*s: restoration, renovation, and remodeling. It is only when you encounter a green granite kitchen complete with Greek pillars, dropped like an off-color joke into the middle of a charming old farmhouse, that you might wonder if there was a stage someone missed in the design process. It's something worth considering, not just to avoid an architectural faux pas, but for what it can teach you about life.

Of the three terms, *restoration* is the strictest. To restore a house means to take it back to what it originally was. In a restoration, the homeowners become caretakers of an older way of life. They live in what is essentially a museum, even heating by the original systems. Windows remain single pane, and damaged plaster is repaired using traditional techniques. Never drywall.

It requires a certain kind of person to live in a restored house. There is a young couple in Port Townsend who fall into this camp. Their house is lit by oil lamps, and you can often see Sarah walking the streets in Victorian garb (including a corset—her waist is a tiny twenty-two inches), or observe Gabriel perched atop his bicycle with its giant front wheel. In many ways, they appear far more natural among the old buildings than the tourists in their yoga pants. Every time I see them, it feels like a glimpse into a town that used to be.

But impressive as such dedication is, Ben and I had no desire to follow their example, or take on a pure restoration. When I hear the word, it reminds me of the story of a young woman in Italy who wanted to learn how to cook a pork roast. Her mother gives her instructions, including one that seems rather strange: cut an inch and a half off the end of the meat before putting it in the pan.

"Why?" the young woman asks.

Her mother shrugs. "That's what my mother always told me. You'll have to ask her."

The question goes up through the generations.

"Why did you cut an inch and a half off your pork roast, Bisnonna?" the young woman finally asks her great-grandmother. The older woman looks at her, equally puzzled.

"That was the size of my pan," she says.

AND THUS, WHILE I AGREE it is important to preserve some houses as museum examples, I don't think we all have to live that way ourselves. Luckily, there are other options.

The middle ground on the spectrum of keep-or-pitch belongs to renovation. For a renovator, a house is not an artifact locked in time, but a distinct being with a character and history that should be upheld, even as the owner's needs are taken into account. In this more synergetic approach, it is acceptable to add a new heating system if it's not obtrusive, or replace old windows with double panes as long as they are similar to the original in style. The intention is a seamless transition between old and new, but as you might suspect, there is a lot of grey area in this approach.

Which jumps us to a fourth *R*, perhaps the most important: respect. For a renovator, respect is not an authoritarian thing; instead, it is an acknowledgment that there are always two sides to an equation. It is a promise to work together to bring out the best in both.

Respect often goes out the window in a remodel. For remodelers, the existing structure is viewed more as a head start on the way to a new house. Want more light? Just slap a bay window in the middle of a wall. Need more room? Go up, or out, in whatever configuration gives you maximum square footage. In my years as a real estate agent, I saw delicate bungalows with second-story additions perched on top like alien spaceships. A spiral staircase dropped in the middle of a living room, because the owners wanted access to the attic. A turret added to a Midcentury Modern, because the husband liked all things medieval. It is the equivalent of fracking on a domestic scale—the need always justifies the means.

There is the argument that, as with fracking, this is the owner's property to develop as they like—and yet I believe that it's not only architecture that suffers when we treat a house as a mere possession. We are diminished as well. There is much that a renovation can teach us about respect and empathy, the weaving of our needs into those of another—even if the other is made of wood. Perhaps especially so. A house is a quiet partner; you have to listen carefully.

IT'S PROBABLY CLEAR THAT of these three approaches, Ben and I gravitated toward renovation. A renovation implies an equal relationship between a house and its humans—and I found the idea of working *with* the house to be far more exciting than working for it, or on it. Not simply because of my obvious tendency toward anthropomorphism, but because I love making connections. It can get messy or complicated, but that's half the point. I wanted to understand our house and what it had to teach me.

AT THE SAME TIME THAT we were making this choice about the house, we were seeing couples around us facing similar decisions with their marriages. Many of us had eldest children in middle school, and after years in the tunnel of raising young offspring, for the first time we were having a chance to look up and around. The partner many saw across the dinner table was not always the person they remembered falling in love with. Or perhaps it was their own needs that had changed. In any case, it seemed that everywhere Ben and I looked, marriages were blasting apart. It was scary.

If marriages are like houses, then it is understandable that sometimes the structure will simply no longer fit. Or maybe it was the wrong style to begin with. But when I looked across the dining room table, I still saw the man I had married, even if our marriage had gone in a different direction than we had intended. There were things we needed to change, but how to accomplish that without destroying what we had would be tricky.

We had one advantage over those other couples, however—we had a big old house full of trash.

AS WE LEARNED THE EXTENT of the work required for the house, Ben and I had to concede that we needed a local general contractor on board. We knew as well, however, that even with a contractor, every house project needs a point person for all the decisions that arise, as well as someone to keep an eye on quality and finances—and that everything goes more smoothly if that contact person is one spouse, not both.

It wasn't a clear or simple decision whether that person should be Ben or me. Ben had a facility with plans, and he knew tools; he'd helped his father build a cabin and worked on a demolition crew for two hot summers in Saint Louis. He had also recently left his job with a big company and was working on his own, which gave him more flexibility. On the other hand, I had overseen projects for our house in Seattle, and I was used to keeping things on budget and schedule while still being a parent.

This time, however, the project was an entire house—two hours and a ferry ride away. No chance to zip back home for a child's forgotten lunch or to be there when they got home from school. If I was to be the point person for the house in Port Townsend, we would need to make some radical shifts in how our current household functioned. I, for one, was ready to see that happen.

Like many people, Ben and I had a different plan for our lives when we began our marriage. We'd met in college; Ben was studying to be a sculptor, and I wanted to be a writer. In those long, delicious conversations you have when you first fall in love, we shared visions of two artist parents with flexible jobs, passing the beautiful batons of our children back and forth through creative and satisfying days.

My own parents had had a traditional marriage—the father goes to work and does important things, while the mother takes care of the kids. With the confidence of a twenty-one-year-old, I was certain that Ben and I could do better. I got into graduate school, and we moved to Seattle, determined to chart our own, new course.

But life happens. While I was busy studying, Ben—who found the reality of a wife with her head in a book remarkably boring—discovered computers. By the time I finally graduated, facing a job market with 350 candidates for every college teaching position, he was working in the software industry. If we chose to prioritize his career, we could stay in Seattle, a city we loved. I could write and be a mother, away from the academia that I had already become disenchanted with. A perfect solution.

And one that quickly began to look eerily like my parents' marriage. I had married a man I thought was as different from my engineer father as possible—and yet at one point in our marriage, Ben not only worked for the same company my father had, he held the same job title. He was the one leaving early in the morning and getting home late; I was the one getting up at night with a sick child so my husband could sleep.

I had wanted children, a longing that had risen in my bloodstream, at times in direct contrast with logic or brain. Before the kids were born, I'd lived in an academic world, my days spent in libraries, searching for authors that time had hidden. I reveled in the deep walls of silence that grew up around me as I sank into my task, how the world outside was replaced by one formed only of thoughts. And yet I'd yearned for something else—brightness, warmth. A life lived in the body and soul as well as in the mind.

My children arrived, and I fell into them. They didn't so much change my perspective as obliterate it. Writing became something I slipped in during a baby's nap or an hour or two of preschool. But the truth was that, even in those excerpts of time, I could never really shut down the listening ear. You could say it was guilt, but just as much it was the desire to catch sight of my son's face as he first woke up, or to hear my daughter's excitement as she told me about her fifty plans for our afternoon. My children reached out for my life, and I gave it to them without hesitation.

Still, at times I could feel it, a steady drip, as if I were leaving a watery trail of myself as I walked through the kitchen, drove the car pool, and made birthday cakes. I loved my children; I loved my husband—but I could not help privately feeling as if I had somehow broken a contract with myself. Whether or not Ben felt the same as he sat in his office—if he yearned to be back in a studio with his hands sliding over arcs and hollows of wood rather than dealing with user interfaces and beta testing—was a question we never had the time or energy to discuss. But now that the kids were thirteen and ten years old, we had a little more flexibility.

The house in Port Townsend had shown up like a big asbestos-covered marriage counselor, forcing the issue. Without realizing it, we had put ourselves in a position that required change. Or maybe we did know it in the back of our minds, just as we must have known, at least a bit, how crazy we were to take on the house at all.

IT WAS A COIN TOSS who would get the job of house project manager, but I was eager to do it. The challenge was exciting, and even if it hadn't been, I was determined not to be left behind at home again.

There was another consideration as well. Our daughter was now an adolescent, a time when mother-daughter relationships are often at their most difficult. We were no exception. When Kate's hormones started cycling together with mine, the males in our household hid under the table, dog included. She and I had always had an issue with who was in charge, from the very first time I tried to convince her that wearing a bathing suit to preschool in the winter was not a great idea.

I worship, often too fervently, at the altar of control; it soothes my mind and brings order to my life. Controlling Kate was like holding water in a colander. She was bold, intelligent—I could see the person she would be as an adult, and it filled me with awe, but this interim period was driving us both crazy.

"You don't trust me to be in the house by myself," she'd accuse me, furious, when I'd come home and trace the dots of forbidden green or blue or orange hair dye that created a trail from the bathroom sink, up the stairs, to her room.

But Ben had a sense of humor, and he liked teenagers. Always had.

"Hair grows," he would tell me. "There's paint for the walls."

While I would sit there, muttering in my martyrdom about who would be repainting those walls, he would just hand the brush to Kate—which made him the far better choice to parent an adolescent.

"YOU SHOULD DO THE RENOVATION," Ben said. "It's your turn. I can handle the kids—and honestly, I can do it better when you're not here."

That was part of what worried me. The one time I had left my little family alone for a week, I had come back to stories of pizza night after night, and a massive cleanup in the hour before I returned. Nobody died, but it wasn't the way I did things.

"If we're going to do this," Ben continued as if reading my mind, "we can't double-parent—on either end. Construction guys will naturally turn toward the guy for a decision; that's just how it is. And the kids will always look to you. We gotta make it clear who's in charge—you're out there, and I'm here."

"Okay," I said, wondering how well either one of us could keep that bargain.

Later, I talked with the kids.

"What do you think?" I asked, watching their reactions carefully.

"Would you live there?" Ry asked.

"No way," I said. "And you'll barely know I'm gone. It'll mostly be while you're at school."

"I think it would be great for you," Kate said, her eyes lit by the possibilities, but whether they were for her or me, I wasn't sure. "Go for it," she said.

Or perhaps, just go.

IN HIS BOOK *WHY WE BUILD*, Rowan Moore presents a fascinating way of thinking about architecture, although his theory could apply just as easily to relationships: "Buildings, seemingly so fixed, are always in motion. From conception to demolition, they are negotiations between the people who make, use, and experience them. . . . They are propositions about the lives they might contain, always subject to revision."

Nothing is static. You can see this in the structures around you as they adapt to their owners' needs. The theory is writ large in warehouses that turn into artists' lofts, a fishing boat that finds new life as a writer's studio, and railroad tracks that become bicycle paths.

There are some structures that are purposefully designed to evolve over time. When the city of Iquique, Chile, wanted to rehouse squatter communities, they hired architect Alejandro Aravena. The budget was tiny, but rather than build flimsy larger structures, Aravena created what he called "half a good house"—narrow three-story linked units with open spaces between the upper floors. He put the money into the kitchens and bathrooms, the most expensive parts of a house, and gave each family just enough room to live in. As the families became able to afford it, the open spaces between the upper floors allowed them to expand for their own purposes. The buildings became an invitation, providing something else that was essential—room for the imagination.

Seen through this kind of lens, our built environments become something entirely different—not static structures, but more like gardens, planted and tended with a patient belief in the future, structures that can give us different views in different seasons, that grow as we grow.

The poet Robinson Jeffers's Tor House provides an inspiring example of this way of thinking. When Jeffers and his wife, Una, discovered the coast of Carmel, California, they bought a piece of land, and over the years, Jeffers built a series of structures there using local stone. First came a small one-story house styled after an English cottage. Later, over the course of four years, Jeffers built Hawk Tower as a gift to his wife and their twins. Incorporated into both structures were small stones from all over the world—from the Great Pyramid of Cheops in Egypt to cathedrals in England—and lava from Hawaii's Kīlauea volcano.

There is something marvelously integrated about these buildings. They seem to come from the ground itself—distinctly human-made and yet part of their surroundings. And their production was equally integrated into Jeffers's life. He would write in the morning and build in the afternoon, letting the work of fitting stone into stone help him plan his poems. He continued this routine throughout his life. In the end, Tor House was a home that grew and changed, created with Jeffers's imagination for his family. I cannot imagine a better love poem.

This is what I wanted in my marriage with Ben, I realized: a stone structure built over decades with hands of love; a warehouse that turns into a space for creativity; railroad tracks that become a path to adventure. When it came to my marriage, I didn't want the restriction of a restoration, the requirement to preserve a structure that no longer fit. But neither did I want the wrecking bar. I wanted a renovation.

Which, of course, leads you right back to that tricky fourth *R*.

Part II:
DIGGING OUT

TRASH

Every house is a living museum of habitation.
—David Owen

OVER THE YEARS, PEOPLE HAVE asked us, usually with confused looks on their faces, why we offered to clean out the house in Port Townsend. For the most part, we just pointed to the simplest reason: it was the only way to move the negotiations along. Many folks assumed we hoped to find treasure, and there was a bit of that—I had spied an antique rolltop desk at the back of the basement as we did our inspection of the house. But what really motivated us was something completely different.

One of the things that binds Ben and me together is our love of stories. We collect stories the way other people do Hummel dolls or beer steins. We line them up on the shelves of our minds, hold them up in varying lights, and see how they change. They are the bones of our family, the warm and moving blood of our friendships, and the telling of them is an art of its own. I'd wanted to be a novelist my entire life, but those everyday stories were the closest I'd ever gotten. They were an outlet for narrative when being an author still seemed so impossible that it felt like someone else's dream.

And so if I am to be honest, I will tell you that when we agreed to clean out the house, it was not for expediency, or the hopes of finding an item that would stun the experts on *Antiques Roadshow*. It was for the stories.

As they say, be careful what you wish for.

WE SET OUT FROM Seattle on a Saturday morning in early February, dressed in our most expendable work clothes. The house had been legally ours for only fourteen hours, but Ben and I were already heading for Port Townsend, taking our children with us, anxious to get in that reluctant front door and start removing trash. It was past time to start taking care of things, to clear out all that was in the way of what could be.

As Ben drove, he and I tried to explain to the kids about the value of working on the house together—home renovation as family bonding. Underlying our words was the subtext, understood by everyone in the car, that everybody else thought we were crazy, but they, our children, would have to help us.

"I think we deserve better than minimum wage," Kate said.

"Who said you were being paid?" Ben replied, shooting her a grin.

"Okay," said Kate, shifting tactics fluidly, "but I get the motorcycles on the front porch." She was years away from a license, but Kate had been yearning to drive since she was born, eager to hit the gas and head off to a life of her own making.

We spent the rest of the trip speculating about what we might find. During the inspection we'd seen a pristine KitchenAid mixer and a covey of antique cameras mingled among the bedlam of objects— and then there was that rolltop desk. Who knew? Perhaps we would find enough to give us a head start toward the renovation. Or at least pay the dump fees.

"I really hope I find a jump rope," said Ry to no one and everyone in particular. "The kind with the wooden handles."

As far as we knew, Ry had never even jumped rope, but I was in no position to call anyone else's desires strange at that point. I looked back, and he gave me a small smile.

"THE MOTORCYCLES ARE GONE," announced Ben as he reached the front porch.

"Damn," said Kate. "All of them?"

We unlocked the front door and made a quick pass through the house. It appeared the heirs had finally found motivation. The big-screen television and the KitchenAid had been carted away. In the bedrooms, dresser drawers had been emptied, the unwanted contents dumped on top of the items already on the floor, like a fresh layer on a compost heap.

Down in the basement, Ben and I looked across the swamp of old boxes and furnace filters and rolls of dirty insulation to a neat, square hole in the back corner, where the antique rolltop desk used to be.

"How the hell did they get that out?" Ben asked. "Teleportation?"

What was left behind was disconcertingly and definitely trash—mountains and days and weeks of it. As we stood there looking, an oily smell slithered in from the furnace room. I peeked in the door and saw dozens of coffee cans filled with a shiny black motor oil, scattered around the floor like a field of liquid land mines. We had seen them during the inspection, but I had been focusing elsewhere. Now, I realized that I didn't even know what to do with used oil, and my utter lack of knowledge suddenly seemed vitally important.

One thing was clear, however. We were in this, and there was no way out but through. I knew with utter certainty that this was more than we could handle—and that we would do it anyway.

"WELL," SAID BEN, TURNING to me. "Wanna get started?"

We went back upstairs, where our children were making their way along the trail through the living room like Hansel and Gretel in a very strange forest, picking up small and fascinating objects. A white ceramic tiger, its snarling face looking back over one shoulder; a miniature Model A car that proved to be a container for bourbon. A pair of wing-tip shoes. A lavender-colored toilet seat. A black-and-white photograph of a child.

"Okay, guys," I declared, hoisting up my box of forty-gallon plastic bags. "Dust masks on. Recycling goes in this bag; garage-sale stuff goes"—I looked around—"on the front porch after we clear it off, and trash goes straight to the dump truck. Everybody got it?"

"Hey, check this out!" Kate had picked up a palm-sized white paper packet from the floor. "Instant Pussy!"

"What?" I asked.

"Just add hot water," she read solemnly.

"A cat?" asked Ry. At almost eleven, he was not far from the age where a small, encapsulated sponge could turn into a giant dinosaur in the water of a bathtub.

"No." Kate's voice held an air of weary superiority. "It's—"

"Hey, Ry!" Ben interrupted from where he was standing next to the couch. "Look at this!"

How he spotted it, I still don't know, but he'd reached down into the depths between the cushions, past decades of newspapers and coats, and was pulling out a brand-new wooden-handled jump rope, still sealed in its cellophane package. We all stared at it for a moment; it seemed entirely plausible that it would simply disappear again.

"Wow," Ry said.

"Why don't you go try it?" I suggested. "Outside."

Ben and I watched until our son was safely beyond the front door, and then turned to Kate.

"Not a chance," she said. "This is waaaaay too interesting."

THERE IS SOMETHING FASCINATING about hoarders. We watch them on cable television shows, slow down as we drive by their houses, as if observing the scene of an automobile accident. Perhaps the most infamous American hoarders were the Collyer brothers, who lived in a three-story brownstone in Harlem in the first half of the twentieth century. When police went to check out a report of a dead body on March 21, 1947, they encountered far more than they bargained for. After failing to get in through any of the entry doors because of the mass of objects behind them, officers finally entered through a second-floor window, where they found a universe of junk that rose eight feet high. They discovered Homer's body first. It took them almost three weeks to find Langley, ten feet away, crushed by the weight of newspapers triggered by one of his own booby traps. Workers took out over 170 tons of trash, including a Model T Ford, a canoe, an x-ray machine, a two-headed fetus, and fourteen grand pianos.

The brothers had come from a wealthy and distinguished family—in fact, one of those fourteen pianos was a gift from Queen Victoria herself. Both brothers went to Columbia University, where Homer was Phi Beta Kappa. Homer studied law; Langley, engineering. But something, obviously, went sideways. Their parents' deaths in the 1920s likely helped trigger their hoarding, but the brothers had already disconnected their phone by 1917. As their world grew smaller, it became dense with possessions. One of the last times anyone saw Homer outside of his house was in 1940, when he was spotted dragging a tree limb inside. Their goal was to be self-sufficient, Langley once said.

IT IS ESTIMATED THAT up to 6 percent of the US population has a problem with hoarding that is serious enough to affect their ability to live normal lives. That means as many as nineteen million people. And yet the desire to acquire is a human trait, shared by many animals as well. According to researchers Randy Frost and Gail Steketee, the way most nonhoarding people feel about their possessions is not that different from someone who hoards. All of us tend to feel responsible for the things we bring into our lives—they help define our identities, give us a feeling of safety, and create a sense of personal history. The difference with hoarders is in scope and intensity.

For a hoarder, each object has its own story, its own many possible uses. Frost and Steketee relate the example of a woman who could not throw away a pen cap because it could potentially be used as a piece for a board game. Some hoarders buy future birthday gifts for people they do not yet know. Still others collect articles that have no particular relevance to their lives, but might be interesting to someone else, someday.

In fact, seen from a different angle, a hoarder's desire to collect and preserve could be perceived as generous, while my need to organize and minimize might be considered overly judgmental. The weekend we spent cleaning out the house made me reexamine my own emotional relationship with possessions—but at that point in time, with only forty-eight hours at our disposal, the only obvious thing to me was that a wheelbarrow is more useful than theories when it comes to getting rid of trash.

"YOU KNOW, MOM," KATE mused as she pulled a Barrel of Monkeys from a warren of shiny graduation gowns and started to make a long orange simian chain, "if the house is tilting anyway, why not just tip it over and dump all this out?"

In actuality, that felt exactly like what had already happened. Across the floor of the living room, pirated porn videos nestled up to religious tracts. Thirty-year-old encyclopedias commingled with cracked bench-press weights and fishing rods and used light bulbs, family photos scattered throughout it all like broadcast fertilizer. It was as if someone had taken the possessions of thirty years of living, from the most deeply intimate to the most profoundly impersonal, dropped them in a huge bag, and shaken it, then poured them, clattering and banging, back into the house. It was unnerving, frustrating, impossible.

"Hey, Mom," Kate said, "are we still doing a garage sale?"

I looked at the ancient handheld vacuum cleaner she was holding up—and its size compared to the monumental task in front of us felt like a textbook definition of irony. I remembered a moment, barely an hour earlier, when I had dutifully plucked a receipt from a cluster of plastic name tags in order to put it in the recycling bag. I had a system, intricate and calming, through which I would create a new world order out of chaos. But it was simply absurd; every pile led to another pile. Did you categorize by genre? Car parts, lingerie, books, toothpaste, passports? Or maybe condition: Dusty, moldy, alive? With so many variables, my mind spun endlessly, looking for a single starting point, but there was none to be found. Nothing made sense.

Never had my need for structure and organization been more obvious. For all our married life, Ben had been trying to get me to concede control—to fate, to fun, to him. In the trash, I had met my match.

"Just pitch it," I said to Kate in frustration.

WE WERE A COUPLE hours into our task when our friend Tom showed up at the front door. In feng shui, they say that a front door located on the right side of the house is the "helpful-people door." At that moment, it was absolutely true.

"Need another worker?" Tom said. He stood there, a box of doughnuts in his hands, his girlfriend's black pickup truck visible in the driveway behind him. I didn't know which I was happier to see.

Ben and Tom and I go a long way back. We met in college, where Tom had arrived after a year at a scientific institution that left him gasping for a bit of liberal arts. Tom is brilliant and mercurial, known for his wide-ranging reading habits and practical jokes. He and Ben get along famously.

When Ben and I moved to Seattle, we stayed for the first week with Tom and his girlfriend, Connie. But while Ben's and my focus quickly narrowed to graduate school and jobs, then babies, Tom and Connie set off on a three-year journey around the world, teaching English in Japan, picking apples in England, biking across the United States. Their letters would arrive occasionally, exotic sound bites on blue aerogram paper, still carrying the faint scents of curry or train travel, and I would read them while breastfeeding a child or formulating some arcane theory concerning nineteenth-century female American novelists.

I could never decide if I wanted what Tom and Connie had, or if I wanted them to come back and have what I did. But it became obvious that neither would happen. Eventually, Tom and Connie did move back to Seattle, but not to have children, and our lives ran in alternate universes, separated by five miles and a whole lot of plastic toys. And yet they were true friends, and when there was a need they were always the first to offer assistance. At the sight of Tom in our doorway in Port Townsend, I could feel my shoulders drop with relief.

"Lots to do," Tom commented, looking about. "Connie's coming tomorrow. Should I start with the dining room?"

And with that, he pulled out a dust mask and went to work.

YOU CAN'T DO JOBS like these without help. Professional assistance, certainly, and we would have that. But what was even more important was the support of those friends who believed in us, who came and dug us out. The friends whose eyebrows never raised, who never cringed in disbelief, who told us they saw the potential in the house even if they didn't. Because, believe me, we had enough concerns of our own. We didn't need a chorus; we needed a team. And we got it.

Connie would arrive on Sunday, a whisper of a woman who nevertheless tackled that camping porta-potty, which was, unfortunately, as full as we had feared. Our friends Reed and Tina would come, too, throwing stained and dusty mattresses out of second-story windows into the dump truck, joking as if it were all a great adventure. They would give us a foundation when truly we had none.

BUT FIRST, WE HAD to get through Saturday.

"Ready for the yuck room?" Ben asked as we finished our lunch.

It had been a quiet affair; no one felt terribly hungry except for Ry, who had spent three hours jumping rope outside. We sat on the front porch steps sucking in the clean, cold air, ignoring how much we had left to do. Even Kate, whose morning had been punctuated by the intriguing discoveries of stacks of *Playboy* magazines and boxes of bullets, was getting tired, slumped against the porch walls, dust mask pushed down around her neck like a cowl. It seemed every time I moved, something fell out of my hair, and I kept my hands as far away from my grimy clothes as possible.

Earlier that day, in an effort to keep ourselves amused, we had started a tally on one wall: *Bowling Balls vs. Rats.* The former had risen up through the assembled detritus on the floor, one after another like a forest of multicolored mushrooms. Their number on the tally list had already reached ten. The rats so far had just been sightings, the fast flash of a tail on the way out the door, but their numbers had been coming on strong. It was hard to convince ourselves to go back inside, especially with the room we knew was waiting.

THE YUCK ROOM WAS the fourth square of our Foursquare house, backing up to the dining room. After considering the layout of the house, it seemed likely it had once been the original kitchen, back before the butler's pantry had been remodeled to take over that function. Now the yuck room was a junk graveyard. Of its three doors, two were completely blocked by piles of objects. The one to the back porch could be opened a slim ten inches. We'd tried pushing on one of the doors earlier that morning and gotten nowhere. It had been easier to put the room off; there was plenty else to do.

But now the rest of the main floor was done. No more excuses. We walked around to the west side of the house. Tom and I started grabbing the stacks of newspapers that filled the back porch, passing them down to Kate and Ry, who carted them to Tom's truck for recycling. When the pathway was clear, Ben moved the dump truck into position and he, Tom, and I switched from dust masks to respirators and jammed our way into the yuck room.

"Holy shit," Tom said.

The window in the room was covered by a piece of cardboard, but in the shaft of light from the back porch, we could just make out a roiling conglomeration of junk. A headless baby doll sat on top, a hand raised in welcome—storage à la Stephen King. At the very back of the room, we spotted a tall white freezer with a lock on the door.

"If there's a body in there, we just stop, right?" I said in an undertone to Ben and Tom.

"You got that right," Tom replied.

"Kids, don't come inside," I said firmly, over my shoulder.

This time, there was no argument.

IT DIDN'T TAKE LONG before our muffled commentary diminished to silence, punctuated only by the occasional shocked blurt of noise. Inside my respirator, the world narrowed to the sound of my breathing, the dim and watery light. I had entered some kind of new and surreal ecosystem, an alternative chain of being: the thing, the box it came in, the remains of what it made, the remains of the thing that ate the remains. A package of bacon, the grease gone iridescent along the edge. A molten bag of bread. A birthday card, dark speckles erasing the words like time itself.

Ben went outside and came back with pairs of goggles, which he distributed wordlessly to Tom and me. My sight was reduced even further to the foggy view through heavy plastic, and the rest of my body followed suit, shrinking back from contact with everything around me. I dove into my head. But the room wanted in, the smells of dust and mold and death pushing against the respirator, the sticky floor grabbing at my feet, objects reaching out to brush against my arms, my back, my hair in invitation: *Come in. Join us. You know you want to.*

"How's it going?" Ry called in the back door.

"*Stay out,*" we yelled in unison.

Even though there were objects worth saving—huge bottles of shampoo, never used; ten-packs of socks still in their original packaging—without even consulting one another, Tom and Ben and I made a pact: everything from that room went away. We bagged, lugged, and pitched our loads into the truck without stopping, without talking, for three hours.

We finally made it to the freezer. The lock was not clasped, and we opened the door.

Inside was elk, in neatly wrapped foil packages. One was dated two years before.

"But how . . . ?" I said.

An hour earlier, Ben had found a child's drawing, done by one of the heirs now fully grown, two-thirds of the way down the pile blocking the freezer. If you followed basic rules of an archaeological dig, those objects must have been accumulating for decades. It didn't make sense. None of it did.

As I shoved someone else's old underwear into a trash bag, an anger swirled up in me that I didn't know I could feel. I was angry with these people. For the way they had treated their house. For the way they had treated themselves. And I was furious with us, because I knew that the only reason we were in that room was because we had practically begged to be allowed to do the job. We'd put ourselves there because we'd thought it might be exciting in some way, a story worth telling. The stories I found in that house, however, just made me want to run.

BUT THERE'S A CATCH to this, as there so often is. All my life I'd wanted to be a writer, and the writers I admire most are the ones who do exactly the opposite of running away. They bravely enter the most hidden parts of human minds, embracing the beauties and tragedies of who we really are. They have an ability to explore the recesses of another's soul in a way that most of us could only dream of achieving.

Some twenty years before that trash weekend, I had gone to see a famous author speak. She talked about her fictional characters—how they became real, took over her books. I found myself yearning for that experience, but it seemed so foreign that I wondered if perhaps her agent had told her to say those things to make herself sound more mysterious.

When I went up to have my book signed, I told her—in that slightly cynical manner of twenty-three-year-olds who don't know any better—that I was a writer, but that no characters had ever spoken to me.

The author looked up and gave me a gracious, if somewhat amused, smile. "Well," she said, "maybe you're not listening."

Sometimes, particularly when you are in a yuck room surrounded by rat skeletons, listening is the last thing you want to do. And yet as writers and, more importantly, as human beings, it is our job to listen even when it is hard. It's too easy to stand on the sidelines, certain we would never allow our lives to descend into such disarray—ignoring the fact that we don't for a minute know what this situation meant for the other person. In fact, given what researchers have learned about hoarders, it could well be that what I encountered in the house was not chaos for the person who lived here. It might have meant safety. Comfort. It was certainly the result of human needs we all share in some degree or another.

Earlier that morning, as I'd stood in that debacle of a dining room, I'd gazed out the window and seen the outlines of the orchard under a sea of ivy, fruit trees planted by someone's hand in a neat double row. Out on the front deck, we'd found a delicately painted ceramic coffee cup, left behind perhaps by someone who had come outside for a slow moment in the sun.

At one point, as I was carrying a bucket full of leaking antifreeze bottles to our hazmat pile outside, I ran into one of our neighbors. I expressed my disgust with the job we were doing, and my frustration with the former owner.

"He was always a really nice guy," the neighbor said, giving me a quieting look.

If I really wanted to be a writer, I understood that at some point—not that day, perhaps, but at some point—I would have to learn to listen. Because here's the thing about great writing, and it's the same as with a successful renovation or marriage—in the end, the most important part is empathy.

"Have we made a day of it, then?" asked Tom. I looked around. The yuck room was empty.

WE SAT AROUND A table at the local pizza restaurant, where they'd welcomed our tired bodies without a single glance at the condition of our clothes. I had marched the kids into the bathroom, where we washed every accessible inch of skin with soap and the hottest water we could stand. Back at the table, the smell of warm cheese and tomato sauce flowed around us. The beer glass in my hand was cold, its contents clean in my throat. It was dark outside, and a few evening tourists walked the main street of town, where little white lights lined the windows of the shops.

"Well, that," Tom said, taking a long and meditative drink, "was what I would call a transformative experience."

I considered what he said as I looked at my children. We had thought it would be hard work, dirty work, the kind that makes you stronger and fills you with an appreciation of your own life and a sympathy for others. But no matter how often we had sent them on errands or out to jump rope, I knew they had learned about a lot more than responsibility, and the realization shook me. If Ben and I had known the extent of what we would find, we never would have brought them. But even with all we had seen during the inspection, we didn't understand—or, perhaps more accurately, could not imagine—what it would really be like. The problem with imagination is that while we like to think of it like a boat, sailing free across an infinite ocean, the reality is that it will always be moored to the dock of what we already know. Our experience that day had extended Ben's and my imaginations. But it had also done the same for our kids.

As parents, we know our children will eventually go out into the world and encounter its variations, good and bad, but that it is our job to protect them while they are with us. Even with the best of intentions, however, things don't always go the way we thought they would. Dealing with the ramifications of those decisions is what makes parenting a job that never truly ends. Sitting there at the table, our kids seemed far more concerned with how long the pizza was taking to arrive than the things they had seen that day, but I knew as well as anyone that all that was part of them now and would be processed bit by bit in the back of their minds for the rest of their lives. The only way out was through.

"What did you think of today?" I asked them.

Our daughter stopped her visual scan of the restaurant.

"It was sad," she said after a moment.

"They had so many furnaces," my son noted. "They must have been cold."

"Who do you think they were?" Kate asked.

"I think you're right," I said. "I think they were sad."

And with that, we started to tell a story.

BY THE END OF the second day, the house was almost empty. As I was headed out with the last of the loads of newspapers, I passed Ben, who was standing on the stairway, a broom in his hand. I looked around me, at the windows barely held in their frames, the plaster warping on the walls, the precipitous slope of the floors. I was dirty and tired, and I just wanted to get me and the kids out of there. But more than that, what Ben was doing seemed futile in the face of the monster projects still to come.

"You're sweeping?" I asked, stupefied.

"Yup," he said, and kept on.

I grabbed the keys to the truck and left, shaking my head.

A half hour later, I returned. As I walked through the dining room, I suddenly stopped. There were the stairs, a clean, ascending line of wood leading up to a pair of six-foot-tall windows on the middle landing. Above me were the sounds of Reed and Tina dismantling one last bed frame; outside, I could hear the kids discussing the best use for the old camper shell in the yard. But there in the middle of the house was one moment of perfect stillness—and in the quiet, I could hear what sounded like the house taking a long, deep breath.

ARCHITECTS AND BUILDERS

Belief in the significance of architecture is
premised on the notion that we are, for better or
for worse, different people in different places—
and on the conviction that it is architecture's task
to render vivid to us who we might ideally be.

—Alain de Botton

WITH THE TRASH GONE, we could finally begin to see the lines of the house. Architects call these lines "bones"—the essential layout of a building, the way the rooms fit one into another.

Our house was built in 1909, after the quest for the railroad terminus failed and Port Townsend changed its expectations. And yet for all that, an American Foursquare is an optimistic, forward-thinking design. Its bones are straight and generous, its main rooms arranged like four strong pillars, with full-height ceilings on both floors. The first-floor rooms open one to the next, while a large landing on the second floor provides a gathering place for the bedrooms upstairs. There is not a single hallway, not an inch of wasted space, and while it is not a big house, it lives larger than its square footage.

IT SURPRISED ME TO learn that the American Foursquare design was influenced by none other than Frank Lloyd Wright. When I think of the sleek rectangular shapes that characterize Wright's designs, the last thing that comes to mind is a two-story square box. But *box* is the operative word here. Born only two years after the Civil War ended, Frank Lloyd Wright knew well the Victorian architecture that characterizes Port Townsend. His goal was to "break open the box" of the small, dark rooms that characterized many Victorians and create floor plans that allowed for easy movement throughout a house. The Foursquare design is strongly influenced by the fluid Prairie style, which shocked the public and helped make Wright famous. For all that our house feels traditional now, at the time its design was a radical departure, inspired by a visionary.

In my experience, architects fall into two categories—the visionaries and the collaborators. The visionaries are the demigods, lifted above us by their unassailable passion for innovation. Their audacity makes sense in a way: architects make shapes out of air, create life from nothing. Their designs influence how you feel as you enter your house, where (and thus how) you eat, the kind of gatherings that will naturally happen or not, and even how inclined you are to have sex. It's a lot of power, and it would be easy to become drunk on it.

When you look at a building like Frank Lloyd Wright's Fallingwater—a masterpiece of concrete and cantilevers that leans out over a waterfall, becoming part of nature rather than passively viewing it from a distance—the structure becomes even more astonishing when you realize it was designed in the mid-1930s, without the aid of the software and building technology that have been developed in the eighty-plus years since then. But Wright was never what you would call a collaborator with his clients, nor did he particularly care if his houses functioned well as homes. His buildings were designed to "human scale," but as he was five foot seven, his houses felt short for some of his clients. And while his floor plans may have been free-flowing, his control of what would occur within them was strict. He designed built-ins, even furniture. In her biography of Wright, Ada Louise Huxtable relates how Wright would sometimes go into "his" houses when the current owners weren't home and rearrange the furniture the way he thought it should be. To Wright, his houses were art, more than places where families would live. When clients complained about roof leaks, which they often did, his response was reportedly a cavalier: "That's how you know it's a roof."

This approach of architect knows best was a hallmark of the Modernists working during that period, and particularly the Internationalists. The Swiss architect Le Corbusier, one of the most famous, confidently asserted that "what [modern man] wants is a monk's cell, well lit and heated, with a corner from which he can look at the stars." Le Corbusier aimed his sights toward a functional future and away from ideas of family or nostalgia. His Villa Savoye is a floating white geometric shape, resting on thin white columns, lifting volume into air. It is otherworldly in its beauty, and utterly antiseptic. Villa Savoye was named a historic monument while Le Corbusier was still alive—an astonishing achievement. And yet, like Wright's Fallingwater, Villa Savoye leaked and cracked. The owners were not, shall we say, universally pleased. As a homeowner, I always find myself thinking of the owners of these structures, even as I remain in awe of the achievement.

And perhaps this is the crux of the issue. Architecture lives in a strange middle land between imagination and reality. To whom does a building really belong? The person who designed it? The public who sees its exterior? Or the client who lives inside?

A striking example of vision over client came from German American architect Mies van der Rohe's design for Edith Farnsworth, a physician who wanted a small second home near a rural creek in northern Illinois. Built in 1951, the Farnsworth House is striking—a glass box, lifted like a prayer above the earth. It was not as peaceful to live in, however. Farnsworth once said, "In this house with its four walls of glass I feel like a prowling animal, always on the alert. . . . I can't even put a clothes hanger in my house without considering how it affects everything from the outside. . . . The house is transparent, like an X-ray."

Van der Rohe sued Farnsworth for outstanding construction costs, which had run far over original expectations. She countersued for fraud. The press and many historians have portrayed her suit as a case of scorned love, gleefully noting her six-foot-tall stature and her "equine features." But I think about that glass house and the feeling of always being watched, not just by what is outside but by the person who designed it, who wanted you to live a certain way. His way. And I find myself siding with Farnsworth.

Perhaps the pinnacle of the architect-centered approach was Deconstructivism. The Vitruvian goals of stability, utility, and beauty were thrown out with the bathwater in this approach. Architect Peter Eisenman's House VI has columns that sometimes don't make it to the floor and sometimes land in the middle of a stairway. One the strangest features is a skylight that flows across the ceiling of the master bedroom, then turns into a narrow window as it runs down the wall, and then continues back across the floor, almost like a glass river. It's thought-provoking and could be admirable, except for the fact that it forces the owners to sleep in twin beds on either side of it. The design wasn't a mistake; it was "postfunctionalism," created to "frustrate normal functions." *Frustrate* being the operative word.

Perhaps it goes without saying that the roof for House VI has been replaced at least three times since the house was built.

IF IT ISN'T OBVIOUS by now, I have a love-hate relationship with visionary architects. Their most experimental works cause me to reconsider gravity and how I see the world, and their contributions as artists are vital to the forward movement of our culture. The problem comes when we try to make homes out of sculptures. And while there are some homeowners who enjoy being caretakers of someone else's eccentric genius, I wanted an architect who worked with me, not above me.

I still remember the day I found Christopher Alexander's *The Timeless Way of Building*. I was in a small bookstore on Whidbey Island, the kind of place where you almost always discover a book that will change your life—although it will likely not be the title you came in to find. *The Timeless Way of Building* is not eye-catching or flashy. Its cover is a soft yellow, and the words inside look like they were written on an old-school typewriter, while the photos are a fuzzy black and white, and of people more often than buildings. Although it was published in 1979, the book feels like a message from even longer ago—but within the space of a paragraph, I was hooked. Through Alexander's eyes, things that I had always instinctively felt about houses became real, solid.

Alexander contends that the primary purpose of a home's design is to make us feel alive—not through acres of granite kitchen counters or sumptuous master bathrooms, but by reinforcing patterns of living that make us our best selves. He studied the ease or discomfort we instinctively feel in buildings and came up with 253 principles that architects can follow. He watched how people settle into rooms with windows on two sides, follow a light down a hallway to its end, rarely use a deck that is less than six feet deep, and avoid courtyards that are almost completely enclosed. He articulated the way porches build communities but also give people an opportunity to shed their public selves before entering a private space. He pointed out that a big room with a high ceiling can make people uncomfortable, but if you add alcoves, or lower a section of the ceiling to distinguish between areas for eating and socializing, people will relax accordingly. According to Alexander, an architect's task is to carefully and deeply observe how we interact with our buildings and then to take that information and create houses that make us feel seen, encouraged, alive.

WHEN I THOUGHT ABOUT our house in Port Townsend, I dreamed of finding an architect who cared about that interactive relationship between home and human. But we had an extra layer to our project, which made it even trickier. Our house was already there, in all its motley glory. A collaborative renovation presents its own challenges, as it is a partnership not only with the clients but with the existing structure. To be successful, an architect needs to respect the original character of the building while at the same time working toward a vision that fits the people who will live within it. The job requires someone who can be part detective, part reader, able to determine subtle patterns in both house and humans, and then use them to integrate new with old. It's a lot to juggle, and yet some people gravitate naturally toward this work, their imaginations freed by constraint rather than limitless possibilities.

Unfortunately, it appeared that all the architects in Port Townsend were booked. I called and emailed, asked for suggestions from everyone I encountered—neighbors, the mail carrier, the guy at the hardware store. No luck. But then one day, while I was at the house waiting for a prospective general contractor, there was a knock on our front door. I opened it, expecting to see a burly builder but was surprised to find a small older man with bright eyes and a close-cropped beard. He looked like an elf, as dressed by Eddie Bauer.

"Hi," he said. "I'm Roman Greggory. Matt, across the street, told me you need an architect."

Maybe feng shui was right, I thought—maybe there was such a thing as a helpful-people door.

Without further preamble, Roman took a quick step into the house, scanning the living room intently. He shook his head in confusion, walked into the dining room, gazed about, opened the door that led to the basement, and then walked back to me.

"Where is it?" he asked.

"What?"

"The front staircase. It should be . . ." He stared at the area that lay to the right of the front door as you entered. That part of the living room had always felt lopsided to me, unsure of its mooring. It had nothing to do with the foundation; it had just felt *extra* somehow.

"There," he said, pointing to the north wall. "There should be a staircase *there*."

The only stairway ascended up through the middle of the house, so narrow and twisting it had been impossible to remove the clawfoot bathtub we'd found discarded in one of the bedrooms. We hadn't been able to figure out how they got it upstairs in the first place. Now, a puzzle piece clicked into place.

"The back staircase was originally for servants," Roman said.

"Why would they take the front one out?" I asked—although perhaps it made its own kind of sense. With no front stairway, the living and dining rooms became obstacles you had to traverse to get to the private upper portions of the house, further separating the inhabitants from the outside world. And while I doubted that had been the owners' conscious motivation, it fit what I had seen of their lives thus far.

Roman shrugged his shoulders, and we gazed for a while at that empty space. I imagined a wide, open staircase greeting you as you entered that front door. The graciousness, the welcome of it. The feeling that there was nothing to hide.

"It would be beautiful," I said.

"Yes," he said. "It's nice to take things back to what they were whenever you can."

We wandered through the house, stopping at the narrow kitchen/former butler's pantry that ran along the west side of the house, adjacent to the dining and yuck rooms. I swung the door open, and we both stared at the space within. We had cleaned it out during the trash weekend, and the plates of desiccated meals, the god-awful stove, and the gnawed-open bags of flour and rice and oatmeal and cake mix had all gone the way of the trash, as had the rats. But that still left the room itself. Leaks in the roof had sent moisture running down the walls and into the floor for years. Every surface was coated with grease. The whole thing felt and smelled like a damp sponge left in the sink for months.

"I don't think you can save this," Roman said. "We're going to need to find another place for you to cook." My heart sank, but part of me was relieved; I couldn't stand the thought of preparing a meal in there.

Where we would now put a new kitchen was another matter, however.

"Don't worry," Roman said. "We've got options."

For the next half hour, we made our way through and around the house, Roman's imagination spinning out ideas. Each one felt like the best combination of us and the house. I signed him up on the spot.

AS ROMAN DROVE OFF, a truck arrived, and George, the contractor I'd been expecting, climbed out. As he walked up the front steps, I could see he had a sturdy build and an open face. I felt an instinctive confidence in him but no sparks between us. *Good,* I thought.

When the experts tell you how to select a general contractor, they usually focus on issues like estimates, experience, licensing and bonding, and references. But as a married woman, I've got a few other criteria that are rarely mentioned. The first is: never be attracted to your builder. In my list of cardinal rules, it's right at the top, because while affairs between an architect and a client have been known to happen, there's plenty of anecdotal evidence that says it's far more likely to occur with a builder. Think about it—a builder is almost always a strong and capable man, working inside your house day after day. He does whatever you ask. He cleans up when he's done. He sees you in the morning in your bathrobe, hears you yell at your kids, and he still comes back the next day. It can be like catnip for women. So I make sure that's a nonstarter, right from the beginning.

The other thing I watch out for is that fourth *R*: respect. Will this man listen to me? Or will he constantly be looking past my shoulder for the man of the house? In my experience, although women are far more likely to be the contact person on a project, it can be hard for them to get complete respect on a job site.

I put out my hand, and George shook it with a grip that was firm and friendly and decidedly platonic. I breathed a sigh of relief and got ready for the next stage.

IF INSPECTORS ARE THE bearers of bad news and architects are the creators of dreams, builders are the caretakers of reality. It is their job to fix what is broken and build what is imagined. Most importantly, however, they deal with how much it is all going to cost.

George and I now took a different kind of tour through the house, a quick fall to earth after scaling the lofty visions Roman had lit up in my mind. But I like the ground, too; at least there, you know where you stand.

"Okay," George said, as we returned to the living room. "Let's talk priorities." From the inspection report, we already knew that the electrical, plumbing, and heating systems were all shot. So were the foundation, the windows, the roof. In fact, it was hard to find something that *didn't* need to be fixed.

When it comes to home renovation, most experts will advise you to put your money into infrastructure and save the fun things like fancy appliances for later, when you can afford it. But infrastructure is even less exciting than maintenance, and it's tempting to put it off. I've seen homeowners do major remodels while ignoring the need for a new foundation—only to watch the house simply collapse from a lack of attention. Cosmetic work may look good, but if your structure is rotten, it's just not smart.

I had a pretty good idea that doing the smart thing here meant there would be no money for a kitchen addition.

"We'll go from the ground up," I said to George, swallowing hard. He nodded, pleased.

"So," he said, gesturing toward the fireplace. "What about the chimney?"

Our chimney. You could see it from blocks away, a thirty-foot-tall tower of smooth, round stones, visually pulling you up the hill. The closer you got, the more fanciful the design appeared: lighter and darker stones arranged in triangles and circles and stars. Local beach rock made into art. You don't see that kind of thing very much anymore; only the very rich, or the most devoted do-it-yourselfers spend that kind of money or time.

The chimney had been one of the things that first attracted me to the house. I loved the whimsicality of it, and I am a sucker for beach rocks. I'd spent my earliest summers in Southern California, amidst the sand and rolling waves. In the Pacific Northwest, it's a little different. In the bays of Puget Sound, the water is quieter, the shore often made of rounded stones. The best Mother's Day of my life was spent hunting for beach rocks with my children and Ben. The ones that contain a ring of white are called wishing rocks, and we collected them, hope made solid.

But I am a person who sees reality as much as hope, sometimes more so. As we had rooted about under the porch during the inspection, it had become increasingly obvious that the chimney was coming apart, due to its location next to the missing downspout. For far too many years, water had been flowing by the chimney and infiltrating the soil underneath—fill dirt, as it turned out, nothing particularly stable. Certainly nothing that should be holding up a thirty-five-thousand-pound chimney. As the ground sank, so, too, did the house, the chimney leading the way like a horse straining against its bit. We were lucky the whole thing hadn't fallen into our downhill neighbor's yard.

"I'd hate to lose it," George said. "It's an important part of the house."

I nodded.

"You can lift a chimney up along with a house." He paused. "But that's when the chimney is in good shape."

As we talked, it became clear that the best bet to save our chimney would be to dismantle and re-create it. Take a picture, tear it down, save the stones, and start over.

"How much would that cost?"

"I'd say you're talking in the tens of thousands."

I knew what George would do; I could see it on his face.

But we didn't have that kind of money—and there was something else to consider. The exterior of the chimney was a wonder, but the interior was decidedly ordinary, with a matte-black painted brick fireplace that commandeered the living room. It looked like our own door to hell, complete with a grimy woodstove crouching in front of it like Cerberus guarding the gates. We could repaint the brick, give the fireplace a new mantel, but it would still always block the light and that hundred-mile view.

"It's your choice," George said.

Restoration. Renovation. Remodeling. Respect.

"What about the plaster?" George asked, tabling the chimney issue for the time being.

I love plaster, too—its texture gives depth to paint and a softened character to walls. But here again, ours was ugly stuff; in the bedrooms upstairs, where the rain had snuck in through leaks in the roof, the ceilings hung down like Miss Havisham's wedding veil, dirty and desperately sad.

"Usually, I'd say keep it," George said, leaning in to examine it more closely. I saw his nose wrinkle involuntarily as he inhaled. "Might make sense to take it down, though. It would make it easier to get to those plumbing and electrical systems."

New plaster and lath would cost a lot of money.

"You can use drywall," George said, sounding a little regretful. "It's still expensive when you're talking about a whole house, but we can make sure you get a smooth surface. It can look nice . . ."

I could almost see him mentally tallying costs in his head. Then he cast his assessing eye on me.

"What?" I asked.

"Well, we're talking about a lot of demolition if all that plaster comes down. You could save money if you did it yourselves."

I couldn't tell if this was a test, a dare, or a reasonable suggestion. In any case, he was right. We hadn't even started, and the costs were already spiraling out of control. We had to cut them wherever we could. I nodded yes.

"Great," George said. "And it *would* be better if it happened before we lift the house."

Now, I was the one doing the mental tally, counting up rooms, walls, ceilings.

"The lighter it is, the cheaper it is to raise," he explained. "Plaster and lath weigh a lot."

"How much time would we have?" I asked.

"I talked with the house mover. He's got an opening in six weeks."

He must have seen the flash of panic cross my face.

"You could use my truck for hauling," he added helpfully.

"Okay." I wasn't sure what else to say.

He turned to leave. "Oh," he said as he reached the door. "While you're at it, you could just get rid of that old kitchen. And it would really help when we do the new foundation if the bottom six feet of asbestos shingles were removed. That will save you a lot."

"Sure," I said.

The door closed behind him, and I sat down, hard, on the floor, feeling it give just slightly beneath me.

PLASTER AND LATH

"Do you see, Pooh? Do you see, Piglet?
Brains first and then Hard Work. Look at it!
That's *the way to build a house."*
—A. A. Milne, *The House at Pooh Corner*

PLASTER IS AN EXTRAORDINARY substance. A mixture of lime, water, and sand or cement, it resists fire, muffles sound, deters termites and rats, and can help control disease. It can be curved and molded, carved into spirals, or laid smooth across a wall. In early America, plaster walls were a sign of social status—in fact, the wooden wainscoting upon which we place such a high premium today was often installed less as decoration than as a way to protect the precious plaster from the rough edges of daily life.

Probably the most extraordinary use of plaster is the frescoes on the ceiling of the Sistine Chapel in Rome. Michelangelo spent four years on scaffolding fifty feet above the floor, paintbrush in hand, face bent upward, inches below the still-damp plaster—his skin soaking up the smell of water and crushed rock as his paint mingled into its damp surface and became color and pattern. It had to be damp, as a fresco can be painted only in fresh plaster, from which it derives its name. But as the surface dries, the paint becomes one with the plaster, making it a remarkably durable medium. The ceiling of the Sistine Chapel was finished in 1512, and it wasn't until the 1980s that a restoration project was undertaken to remove the centuries of grime and candle smoke that had accumulated. The frescoes beneath were still stunning, brilliant in their colors.

ALMOST ALL NEW HOMES in the United States are built using drywall, or Sheetrock—giant pieces of prefabricated material that are screwed into the studs by workers who move at lightning speed and always seem to smoke cigarettes. Plaster walls, in contrast, are expensive and time-consuming, created from a tricky combination of plaster and what is called lath—thin strips of wood nailed across the wooden studs of a building, leaving quarter-inch spaces between them. The plaster is then spread across the lath, oozing through the gaps, which helps adhere it in place.

After several coats of increasingly fine plaster, the wall is smooth—not quite as smooth and consistent as drywall, but that is exactly the point. There is a living feeling to plaster. It accepts paint into itself in a way that drywall never will. It's why our attempts to re-create the elegant, faded appearance of an Italian villa in a modern American home will only ever look like a fake movie set. Not just because that villa is likely centuries old, but because drywall lacks the give-and-take, the generous acquiescence that begins the moment paint is applied to plaster. Plaster walls allow for what the Japanese call *wabi-sabi*—the beauty in transience, the recognition of the aging process that is always present within life. They are a lesson in humility and grace.

Unfortunately, our walls had left *wabi-sabi* behind long before and descended into true decomposition. Water stains spread in alluvial plains from leaking window ledges above; ragged cracks chased each other from corner to corner. From what we had seen, the plaster wasn't doing a thing to deter rats, either. And then, of course, there was the smell—an olfactory distillation of everything we had found as we cleaned out the house.

So, yes, the plaster had to go. But taking down all the plaster and lath in a 2,200-square-foot house in less than six weeks is a sizeable commitment. Luckily for us, we had help.

"The whole house?" the kids asked in astonishment. "What are you going to pay us?"

I was noticing a certain theme to our conversations.

But this job, Ben and I rationalized, was a chance for real family bonding, without the unsettling trash. This would be pure hard work, the kind that builds muscles and character—and on that weekend we would be expanding our family to include Kate's friend Rebecca, a teenager of diminutive size but plenty of energy.

AS WE DROVE UP the hill toward the house, I saw that George's crew had constructed a chute, running from a second-floor window down the outside to where Marge, the company dump truck, was parked. I breathed in a lungful of gratitude. That simple chute would save us hours, if not days, of time, allowing us to empty our second-floor loads in one exhilarating tip-and-spill rather than trudging downstairs over and over with loaded buckets.

We parked, and all of us bailed from the car, glad to stretch our legs after the two-hour drive. As the kids stood around, trying to remember which end of a dust mask was up, George arrived in his pickup truck. He cast his eye over our crew with a bemused expression, but, always supportive, he simply unloaded a collection of tools we were going to borrow in addition to the big dump truck.

"I want this one!" Ry declared, picking up a sledgehammer almost as tall as he was.

"So," George said, drawing our attention, "there are two ways to do this. You can knock down the plaster first and then rip out the lath with a crowbar. That's neater and makes for an easier cleanup. You just scoop up the lath, and then shovel out the plaster."

The kids listened intently. There was more coming; they could tell.

"Or," George continued, "you can just take a sledgehammer and go for it. It makes a mess, but it's a lot quicker."

Kate and Rebecca grinned at each another.

"You might want to start with something a little smaller," George said to Ry, nodding at the sledgehammer; then he hopped in his pickup. "Good luck!" he said. "Call me when you need the truck taken to the dump."

WHEN YOU THINK ABOUT it, we all fall into categories. When it comes to plaster, there are separators and there are smashers, much as in cooking there are those who clean up as they go and others who leave towers of used pots and pans and trails of carrot peelings in their wake. Separating, which requires much less upper-body strength, seemed an appropriate choice for most of our crew, myself included. But as I was listening to George, I'd found myself yearning to be a smasher, no matter how out of character that would be for me.

I was born the youngest of four daughters, who arrived in rapid succession, with a brother eight years later. The ocean of our family was full enough; as a child, it was my job not to cause waves. Every year, when my mother gave each of us a new Christmas tree orna-ment, mine was almost always an angel—reading, cooking, or simply gazing out with sweet, untroubled eyes. Over time, they populated the tree, a phalanx of halos and wings that stayed sedately closed. When I was young, my mother told me a story about when she was twelve, approaching adolescence. Her mother had said with a wry smile, "I think we'll just skip that part." The expectation, passed down through the generations, was clear to me. So I don't yell. I don't hit things. And I have always been someone who cleans up as she cooks.

My daughter, on the other hand, came out of the womb ready to run a small country. She was forthright and headstrong in her emotions in a way I could only dream of being. I refused to constrain her the way I had been, and yet I also felt I had to be an adult and keep her within reasonable boundaries. It was a tricky place to live as a parent, stuck between responsibility and envy, and neither Kate nor I thrived there.

A couple days earlier, I had called my mother and told her about our plans.

"You're going to do what?" she said. "But you're the one who likes things clean and neat."

I was forty-two years old and more than ready to demolish a few expectations. Perhaps, I thought as I considered the tools in front of me, if I could wield a sledgehammer I could become one of those people who rips the wrapping paper off presents guilt-free, or indulges in loud and quickly forgotten arguments—or who maybe, just occasionally, says what she wants. I would take that.

BEN AND THE KIDS and I were arranged around the upper landing, each facing a different wall. Music from an old rock station blared out of our decrepit boom box, with a loud, strong bass beat that demanded destruction.

"Ready?" the kids yelled, hammers and crowbars raised, like cavalrymen preparing for the charge.

They were itching for demolition. I thought of how many times I had reminded my children to be gentle and kind, explained that human beings were meant to create, not destroy. How often had I admonished them as toddlers for knocking down a friend's block tower or obliterating their own Play-Doh creations? It seemed odd now to be handing them wrecking tools.

And yet, I liked the feel of the sledgehammer in my hand.

"Go!" Ben and I shouted.

The kids aimed at their walls and let their implements of destruction fall.

"Yay!" they cried out.

Under the force of their blows, threadlike cracks skittered across the surface of the walls; particles the size of pennies fluttered to the floor. A bit of lath, shy and embarrassed, peeked out. This continued for twenty minutes or so.

Our intentions were good, and Ben, who had done demolition before, obviously knew what he was doing, but at the rate the kids and I were going, we would be hanging our Christmas stockings on lath nails. We needed new motivation, something to put some force behind our tools. I turned to Kate and Rebecca, whose adolescent emotions had begun rocketing about our house like heat-seeking missiles gone astray. It was time to harness some of that power.

"Okay," I said. "What makes you angry?"

My daughter looked at me, considering. Rebecca smiled.

"Really?" Kate said.

I took a deep breath. "Sure—pick a good one, and go for it."

Kate's eyes brightened at the possibility. There was a pause while we all thought, searching for the right choice in our databases of resentments and frustrations. Even with only a few minutes of experience in demolition, I could tell that the energy stored in petty annoyances—the missed green lights and the muddy dog tracks across the living room rugs of our lives—would provide at best a half hour of fairly unproductive work. If you wanted the kind of power that would take down a wall, you had to dig down into areas made murky with willful repression. You had to use anger, rage even, the kind that takes up lodging in your muscles, twisting its way into the fabric of your life.

I could tell from Kate's face when she'd found her choice of motivation, a certainty as clear as love at first sight. Her eyes focused; her mouth set in an expression so grown-up it took me aback.

We hefted our tools, shouted into the air, and heaved. The walls exploded in a glory of white. We kept going. The world seemed made of noise—deeply pitched thuds, hammers hitting home, hoots and bellows. We paused, gasping and laughing. I looked over and saw my son, hammer raised.

"This one's mine," he said, pointing to the wall in front of him, and grinned.

I FIGURED THE CHILDREN would last five minutes; I figured I would last five minutes. The sledgehammer in my hand was heavy. Each time it made contact, shock waves rolled down my arms and legs, a visceral reminder that I had a body, muscles, a life in the physical world. As I pounded, my lungs pushing the air through me like bellows, my thoughts went deeper, subterranean. I was ten years old, stretching my newly long legs, flying along the school track and finishing in a rush of joy—then watching as the boys I'd beaten shunned me, one by one. I remembered biking as a teenager, a car coming up, pushing me off the road, the young men leaning out the windows, their faces wide, greedy. I remembered the feel of my sixty-five-year-old college mentor's thick tongue as he stuck it into my mouth. The advice I was given afterward by a well-meaning older woman: to confront him but to say perhaps I had been mistaken, that this is what I *thought* had happened, and if it had happened, what I would do. Putting him on notice while allowing him an out. A tightrope of compromise— dependent upon my fallibility. As if that saliva-soaked moment could ever be mistaken. As if *his* reputation were the only one that mattered.

My sledgehammer crashed into the wall, and a huge chunk of plaster went flying. The next hit cracked a fault line across the wall. Lift. Slam. I could feel parts of me, hidden, hardened, almost calcified, breaking off and working their way out. I kept going, my muscles stretching, bones grinding. The work demanded deep, heavy breaths; I grabbed air through my dust mask and expelled it in short, hot bursts. Lift. Slam.

Ten minutes later the wall was gone. Gone. Only the studs left behind.

Yes, I thought.

PANTING, I RAISED MY goggles and looked around.

Across the landing, Ben was swinging his sledgehammer in a smooth, practiced rhythm. Ry's wall was half-destroyed, and Rebecca was matching him heft for heft. On a board positioned some five feet above the stairs, Kate stood, pounding at the plaster near the ceiling. Beneath the force of her blows, the wall was crumbling.

I paused to catch my breath and watch my daughter as she worked—our girl, whose soul is lit by fireworks, who fights like a warrior against whatever seeks to hold her back, including me. Watching the force behind her blows, the sheer determination, I could see that while I was the one who'd wanted to be a pioneer as a child, it was my daughter who would have thrived in that environment. Of all of us, it was she who would have had the force of character to build a house out of a forest or get a wagon over a roadless mountain. And it was she who would have the strength to face what had bent my spirit when I was young, if I didn't stifle hers first. If I could figure out which of my boundaries were truly necessary for her safety, and which were like the wings of the ornament angels—hinting at future flight while delivering only a lesson in gravity.

Standing there with a sledgehammer in my hand, I understood that this was the first time that we had truly called upon all of Kate's strength of both mind and body, used its full potential, been grateful for the gift—and her pioneer's heart would know that. She could take that feeling and let it live in her muscles, where anger had been. Maybe we all could.

Our daughter's long, strong arms lifted and smashed her hammer into the wall, letting out all she held inside her safe and regulated life, claiming her role in our future. I had never seen her look so beautiful.

THE HEARTH

To the English, to remove the fire-place
from the home would be like removing
the soul from the body.

—Hermann Muthesius

OF ALL THE PARTS of a house, perhaps the hearth is the most symbolic. Its history goes back to the very beginning of shelter, which was created as a way to protect precious fire as much as the people who gathered around it. When Richard Weston wrote the book *100 Ideas That Changed Architecture*, his choice for number one was the hearth. In Latin, the word for hearth is *focus*, and even now, in our era of radiant flooring and central heat, a typical American child's drawing of a house will include—along with its peaked roof, single door, and two windows—a chimney.

The truth is, the fireplace as a heat source was outclassed in the early 1740s with the invention of the Franklin stove. But we don't seem to care. Even Frank Lloyd Wright, that disrupter of the architectural status quo, still tended to center his houses on a chimney, and in the course of his career he designed more than a thousand fireplaces. When I was doing real estate over half a century later, I found my clients designating a fireplace on their list of "needs" more often than "wants," even in a metropolitan area that routinely banned burning due to air quality concerns. A fireplace means home.

And now Ben and I were going to get rid of ours. It was a practical, rather than aesthetic, choice—still, the thought of destroying our chimney broke my heart. I kept thinking of the person who had spent all those hours making the designs in its stones, a story winding thirty feet up to a heart at the top. Our equivalent of petroglyphs.

If only the person who had built the foundation underneath, and the owners, who were supposed to maintain it, had been so careful. Gravity will always win, and as the foundation had weakened, the chimney had become our personal Leaning Tower of Pisa, its massive weight pulling the house along with it.

It was an untenable situation, but removing it raised the question: What is a home without a fireplace?

BEFORE CHIMNEYS WERE INVENTED in the twelfth century, fires were located in the middle of what was often a one-room dwelling, the smoke rising up to a hole in the roof, fumigating the storage loft above. The smoke was helpful in some ways—it helped preserve meat, and discouraged insects and birds from taking up residence in thatched roofs—but it limited houses to one story. The ground floor was smoky enough, thank you very much.

The invention of the first chimney was nothing short of an architectural miracle, but as with many inventions, this one had unintended social consequences. The ability to locate a fireplace on a wall cleared the air, but it also meant buildings were no longer restricted to one floor, and as they rose, the dynamic within them changed. The early homes had been egalitarian by necessity—family, servants, and often even animals cohabitating in one room. With the possibility of separated living areas, however, classes divided along with the space. The homeowners moved upstairs, and as Bill Bryson writes in *At Home*, "Servants stopped being part of the family and became, well, servants." Personal space was suddenly a concept for the wealthy, and "soon," Bryson writes, "it wasn't merely sufficient to live apart from one's inferiors; one had to have time apart from one's equals, too." It's funny, or not, to think that the origin of our modern-day demand to "give me some space" had its origins in a wholehearted desire to quite literally breathe freely.

Those early two- and three-story houses were drafty and cold, however—and the reality was that the old-style hearth had produced more warmth. For those other than the truly wealthy, who could afford to heat several rooms, the kitchen fireplace continued as the place to gather—until modern central heating was invented in the 1890s and then became a more affordable option in the United States in the 1920s.

Central heating continued the social trajectory that chimneys had begun, scattering families even further, into personal spaces with doors that shut. Later, television would offer its own reason for families to gather, but then technology would disrupt it all again with the invention of personal computers and smartphones. Now the glow most of us are drawn to comes from small screens held in our hands.

And yet there is a part of us that still longs for that feeling of togetherness, and a hearth is the symbol of an earlier time when family members gathered around a fire that held a dangerous world at bay. Inside its warmth and light, we are safe. The ability to keep it burning gives us a feeling of competence. In the end, we are all Neanderthals, thrilled by the miracle of fire.

BEN AND I HAD run the numbers over and over, and saving the chimney was impossible. The initial estimates for the foundation alone were just short of terrifying, and the engineer was still figuring out how to get around the issue of the fill dirt. We knew those early numbers would only rise.

And money was becoming a major issue. Back when we were in the process of buying the house, all the banks had refused to give us a loan, given the state of the foundation and roof. They'd told us to come back later, when those items were done—as if that giant middle step were a mere skip on a hopscotch court. But by that point, we were emotionally committed. After half a year of negotiations, we were damned if we were going to let someone else have our house.

We'd had one other option: our retirement fund. It consisted almost entirely of a high-tech stock we'd bought on a suggestion from a friend. The stock had proved to be an astonishing investment, vaulting from pennies to dollars, like Jack's beanstalk heading for the sky. It'd seemed foolhardy to sell it, and yet we had, riding the wave of emotion. But that decision left us with no cushion for mistakes, no future except for this crumbling house. And while that initial leap had been exhilarating, the stress was starting to show, each new estimate from George ratcheting it higher.

So the chimney had to go, and we had to be the ones to do it, because our labor was free—a simple mathematical equation. Except that what most people tend to forget is that math is done by humans, and humans are rarely simple.

FOR ALMOST SIX WEEKS, we'd worked weekends as a family, demoing the plaster and lath. Increasingly, as the deadline approached and the number of remaining walls stayed stubbornly high, we'd added weekdays for Ben and me, taking turns while the other parent stayed in Seattle with the kids. Ben and I would pass each other at the car door.

"I left dinner in the fridge," I'd say, heading toward the ferry.

"There's two walls left in the living room, but I got the dining room done," he'd reply.

In an ironic way, it was the living incarnation of our original vision of parenting—the two of us as equals, passing the baton of our children back and forth. Except it wasn't. What we were handing off was a house, and like cleaning out the trash, the job was more than we could do. Yet once again, we were doing it anyway, and the pressure was manifesting in quiet but persistent ways: the laundry that was stacking up, the food that increasingly came from a package. The other work, the work that made the money to run our household, was going neglected, along with the kids, whose moods swung from supportive to frustrated. Our marriage we weren't even thinking about, in the way that two cart horses simply move forward together, grateful only that there is another animal in the harness next to them. We just have to get through this, we'd say, and put our heads down and plow ahead, blinkered to the consequences.

It was the end of March now, and we had one weekend left before our house would be lifted off the ground. So far, we'd taken out ten and half tons of plaster and lath. Now we had forty-eight hours, a thirty-five-thousand-pound chimney to demo, and a kitchen and back porch to cut from the side of the house. Oh, and we needed to pry off the bottom six feet of asbestos shingles around the entire exterior.

PERHAPS THE GREATEST IRONY of the whole situation was that in our search for a slower way of living, we had fallen precisely into the trap of the American work ethic. While in the 1970s, the number of hours that Americans and Europeans labored was roughly similar, that has changed dramatically in the decades since. According to a 2016 study, Americans now average 25 percent more work hours per week than Europeans—a number that increases dramatically in the tech industry that dominates Seattle. The game is a competitive one there.

Perhaps it was the influence of this culture, perhaps it was the result of our good Germanic upbringings, but Ben and I fell into this trap more easily than many. When asked "Can you . . . ?" we always took the question literally—as in, physically, logistically, could we do whatever was asked of us? We never changed the question and asked ourselves if we *wanted* to do it. We simply grabbed our overstuffed calendars to see if the new obligation would fit. The bigger the challenge, the better.

When it came to my part in this dynamic, I tended to blame my mother, as children are wont to do. It was she who'd read me *Mike Mulligan and His Steam Shovel* when I was young. Written by the author of *The Little House*, that equally influential book of my childhood, *Mike Mulligan* was another protest against the influx of technology and social change. But while the little house waited patiently for someone to save it, Mike Mulligan tilted like Don Quixote at the windmill of progress. When the big, fancy machines were going to dig the hole for a brand-new building, Mike Mulligan declared that he and his steam shovel, Mary Anne, could do it in one day—an impossible feat for such an antiquated machine. And yet dig they did, through pages of illustrations depicting heroically blowing dust and dirt, with an ever-growing crowd gathering around the barriers, urging them on to victory. I've basically approached my life like Mike Mulligan ever since, although I doubt that was my mother's intention.

What I always forget, however, is that when Mike Mulligan and Mary Anne finished their task—the hole square and neat and deep—Mike realized that in his haste he had forgotten to leave a ramp for Mary Anne to get out. And so Mary Anne is turned into the furnace for the building, with Mike Mulligan sitting beside the flames of her boiler, smoking a pipe. She becomes the hearth, the heart of the structure. Depending on how you interpret the scene, she is also stuck.

I WAS ALREADY OUT at the house when Ben and Ry arrived that Saturday morning. When I saw only two of them get out of the car, I raised an eyebrow at Ben.

"Kate wanted to stay in the city at Rebecca's house," he said. "She's worked hard. I told her she could have a break. She'll lock up the house on her way out."

I stood there trying not to say what had jumped into my mind. But it was hard. I had an ironclad rule with myself: no child, not even a responsible almost-fourteen-year-old, was left to close up our house if an adult was not returning within a few hours. I figured that nothing too bad could happen in a couple hours. But two days? The possibilities were endless.

"Really?" I said. Apparently, I was unable to keep my part of our pact not to second-guess each other.

"Yup," Ben said, putting on safety glasses. "She'll be fine. I'm going to get the asbestos shingles off the kitchen. Ry, you help your mom with the chimney."

Ry looked at me askance.

I shrugged. "Power tools, big guy," I said.

"Can I use them?"

ONE OF THE THINGS that first attracted me to my husband was his sense of well-earned confidence and the feeling I got that he would always treat me as an equal. It pushed me to be a stronger person, and besides, exciting things tend to happen around someone who stretches life's boundaries. When he applied this same attitude to our children, however, it gave me pause—and when I didn't treat them with the same level of confidence he did, it drove him nuts.

Whether we like it or not, most parenting is heavily informed by how we were raised ourselves. In my family, we were expected to be careful, stay safe. And we were—among the five of us kids, there was not a single broken bone or arrest. We girls barely even had boyfriends.

Ben's family was different. They believed in independence and self-reliance. When Ben was thirteen, his parents traveled to the remote jungles of New Guinea to do psychological evaluations of missionaries—leaving the kids in charge of the house for three weeks. Ben's older brother was sixteen, his sister fourteen. There were neighbors and grandparents who looked in on them occasionally, but it was *Home Alone*, the early version. The fact that no one in his family sees anything unusual in this, even now when people seem to have Child Protective Services on speed dial, says something.

I can never decide if I am horrified or thrilled by that story. On the one hand, my husband has a can-do personality that is grounded in real experience, and it makes my life better every day. But there is another part of me that reacts to that story with a looping mental audiotape that basically goes, *Oh my god, oh my god, oh my god.*

As I grew up, I took my childhood training seriously. I wore my seat belt. I never swam alone. When I traveled, I left behind any jewelry it would break my heart to lose. And then I had children, and suddenly, all my cautions were lit in neon. Those two beings were the most astonishing thing that had ever happened to me. They were life itself. When Ben would take us on hikes along steep and narrow trails, my spine went cold as I imagined what could happen to them. For me, the risk was too great.

But Ben would argue that there was a risk in either case. You risked broken bones by letting your children out of the box, but you risked something even more awful by keeping them in it. His mother had let him bike across the country when he was seventeen. He was the better for it, he always told me.

Yes, I would reply. *You can say that now because nothing happened.*

And so we went, back and forth, me protecting the kids too much, Ben stepping in and giving them more slack. Our new parenting arrangement had only made the difference between us more obvious. Up until recently, Ben had mostly been a Saturday–Sunday parent, at the office during the week. Now with him working from home, and me often in Port Townsend, the lid was coming off the box.

BEN WAS OUTSIDE REMOVING the asbestos shingles, while Ry and I were inside on the second floor getting ready to demo the chimney. I was holding a power chisel that George had lent me, a compact machine with a three-foot-long piece of metal that ended in a wicked triangle, the whole thing connected by a hose to a bright-blue air compressor the size of a large Rottweiler. The phallic implications were unmistakable. But then again, most of construction, and certainly the vast majority of demolition, carries the distinct whiff of testosterone.

In the past, that might have given me pause, but I was finding I liked the feel of the new muscles in my arms, the knowledge that I could heft a sledgehammer and make a wall disappear. When I looked in the rearview mirror of the car before heading home, some days I'd barely recognize myself, covered in dust. And I was just fine with that.

WITH RY AT MY side, I aimed the chisel blade into the interior brick of the chimney and depressed the lever. The chisel jumped in my hands, and I bore it into the dry mush of mortar, focusing its energy. The destruction came in long bursts, a *bang-bang-bang* that popped a brick free in one quick volley before I moved on to the next, while Ry dutifully stacked them on the other side of the room. The speed and power of the machine was exhilarating. After weeks of hammering at walls, finally there was progress you could really see, as fast as you could move.

"Mom, can I try?" Ry said every time I turned off the chisel.

I think using an air-powered chisel is the closest a pacifist can get to firing a semiautomatic weapon. I had never even let my children have toy guns, and I wasn't sure I wanted my son near this thing. But there was another, selfish, aspect to my decision here—I knew how much faster the task would go if I was doing the work. And the amount of work we had left to do was a looming thing, ever-present, the list never satisfied, never completed, our deadline two days away.

"Hold on, buddy. You'll get a turn in a minute."

An hour later, Ry was fading fast. The chimney was coming down, but so was his mood. I looked out the window and saw Ben rounding the corner, carrying a stack of asbestos shingles.

"Mom, can I try?" Ry asked again.

I looked at my son and the pile of bricks he had made. Stacking bricks is mind-numbing work, especially for a kid who really wants to be using power tools. I thought of how the past few weeks had taught me to see myself as someone strong and capable. I thought of how much it meant that Ben believed in my ability to do this job—and what it might mean for Ry if I gave him that same gift. Then I thought of what would happen if that chisel slipped in my son's hands just once.

WHEN RY WAS A baby, he loved to perch in a pack on my back as I cooked, his toes pushing against the rail of the pack so he could stand, craning his head over my shoulder to watch what I was doing. I would breathe in his baby smell, along with the scent of garlic, or chocolate, or scrambled eggs. I would describe each step of what I was doing in a language he did not yet understand, and he would respond in a language I never would.

He was my baby, the shy one, whose blue eyes were startling and full of wonder. I wanted to hold him close forever, and so I did, for far too long.

The previous summer, as our family had stood on a rocky beach around a bonfire, Ry asked if anyone would go out in the canoe with him. Ben told him he was old enough to go by himself now and explained what he needed to know in order to manage the boat on his own. I stood on the sidelines, chewing the inside of my mouth. I didn't want my ten-year-old son to go out there alone in our only boat. Even in summer, the water in Puget Sound is deadly cold, and a tipped canoe is no small matter.

I watched as our son pushed off and paddled to the middle of the bay. Then he sat for a long time, looking down into the water, up at the evening sky. Being only himself.

It was time to let him grow up.

"OKAY," I SAID TO Ry now, and handed him the chisel. "Aim for the mortar, not the brick."

"Don't you think I've been watching?" he asked. But he smiled.

The jump-back of the motor startled him, but he gripped the machine with determination. His eyes scanned the chimney, figuring out places of weakness before he aimed. The first brick came out easily, then another and another. He made it through the brick to the open flue, and beyond it, to the other side. There, the lines of mortar were less distinct, weaving around the irregular shapes of the stones. Ry loosened the mortar several stones down, then worked his way up both sides of a chunk of six or so. When it seemed ready to give, we yelled to make sure Ben was out of the way below, and then we pushed with both hands and all our weight.

The chunk let go and plummeted twenty feet to the ground. A patch of sky entered the room. I looked down at the scattered stones.

Someday, I will do something with them, I promised the house, although I had no idea what that might be.

Ry was jubilant, grinning at the hole in the chimney. "Yes!" he crowed. "We're doing it!"

I looked at my son, standing there dusty and triumphant, bursting with confidence.

It's all right, I told myself. *You can let him go. You can let the lid off the box; it'll be okay.*

I could feel the house starting to shift, adjusting, as the weight of the rocks and bricks left it, stretching like a bear coming out of hibernation. I wanted to stop and listen, to feel what was happening and watch my son's exuberance, but there was so much left to do. We were twelve feet down in the chimney; we had twenty-three to go. Ben hadn't even started to cut off the kitchen. We'd never get it done that weekend, I thought. Ben or I would have to stay and keep going until it was finished.

"Good job, bud," I said. "Back to work."

AS RY GOT READY to turn on the chisel again, I heard my cell phone ringing, deep in my pocket. I dug it out and saw Kate's name on the screen. I clicked through.

"Mom? Don't worry. It's all okay now."

"What's okay? Are you all right?" Adrenaline blasted through my body.

"Don't worry. Rebecca's mom is here, and it's not burning any-more—I just wanted you to know."

"*What's* not burning?"

"The house—well, no, just the carpet, really. Rebecca and I were playing with the lizard before we went over to her house. We put him back, but I guess we forgot the heat lamp."

"You left it on the carpet?" There was steel in my voice. It did not sound loving, even though I could feel every molecule of my body trying to transport itself to her side.

"Yeah, I know. Anyway, we went for a walk, but we came back—we did. I just had this feeling. And it's not a big hole in the carpet, I mean, it's down to the wood and stuff, but Rebecca's mom soaked it really well. We're going to her house now."

I was having trouble focusing; I grabbed at the most concrete thought in my head. "Turn off everything electrical before you leave, okay? And check the stove."

"I already did, Mom. Don't worry." Her voice was practical. "See you on Sunday." She hung up.

"What happened, Mom?" Ry was watching my face.

"Everything's fine. Why don't you go find your dad and tell him it's time for lunch."

Ben came up the stairs a few minutes later.

"Ry said there was something with Kate?"

I was sitting on the floor with my back propped against the wall, staring at the ruins of our chimney.

"You left her to close up the house." My voice was made of stones.

Ben immediately went on the defensive. "You wanted me and Ry out here quick. She wasn't ready to go to Rebecca's, so I told her she could lock up. She's almost fourteen."

"She almost burned it down."

It was a horrible way to tell him, and I wasn't proud of it. But I was so angry. I was furious with him for breaking a rule that wasn't even his, angry at him for leaving our daughter in a situation where the ramifications could have been so huge. And I was mad at my daughter for not putting the damn heat lamp back on the top of the cage. For being a teenager. For being human. But mostly, I was scared, in a way I had never been before.

Every time I left the house in Port Townsend, I would think about all the things that could happen to it while we were gone. A windstorm, vandals, fire. There were so many options at least it kept my nightmares from repeating themselves. But in all those scenarios, the house in Seattle was okay; my children were okay. The Port Townsend project was a risk, but it was a contained one, separate geographically and psychologically from my family. Now, suddenly, it wasn't.

I couldn't look at Ben. I knew he was standing there as exhausted as I was. I understood that he had just been trying to give our daughter a sense of independence and responsibility, the kind his family had given him. But I was so angry—it was hot and cold, and filled every inch of me. And Ben and I didn't know how to fight. We'd both grown up the peacemakers of our families, and now we avoided conflict like electricians do a live wire. We had no tools for this.

Once again, we had done this to ourselves. We'd taken on an impossible deadline, gone at it with the energy it takes to build a company, get up a mountain. But we were trying to build a family, and that is a different thing.

"Mom," Ry yelled from downstairs. "Are we getting lunch? I'm starving."

"Coming," I called back. I hoisted myself from the floor and walked past Ben without speaking.

As I approached the open front door, I saw George coming up the porch stairs.

"Hey," he said. "I thought you'd want to know. The lift job before yours just got pushed out. You've got another three weeks for demo now."

I didn't know if I wanted to punch him or hug him.

Part III:

DIGGING IN

FOUNDATION

Do you wish to rise? Begin by descending.
You plan a tower that will pierce the clouds?
Lay first the foundation of humility.
—Saint Augustine

A HEARTH MAY BE THE HEART of a home, but a builder knows that the most important element is the foundation. A foundation calls forth no nostalgia and is rarely featured in the glossy design magazines, but without one, nothing else matters. The moment it cracks, things start to shift.

In the weeks that followed our almost-fire, I seemed incapable of either straightforwardly reprimanding my daughter or reassuring her that I loved her, my mixed emotions coming at her in brief asides like poisoned darts, light but deadly. It was a way I had never wanted to parent, and yet that was my fallback whenever things got tense. I couldn't say what I wanted, couldn't be angry out loud—but like water, anger will always find a way to escape. Kate apologized, over and over, and I would say it was okay, but I couldn't let it go. And I still couldn't talk about it with Ben, who had retreated into an inner sanctum of defensiveness. We threw ourselves into work instead. We pounded and hauled, ignoring what was right in front of us. The fact that every night in Seattle I would go upstairs and see the round singed hole in the carpet didn't help matters. I covered it with a book.

"Are you doing okay?" a friend asked me over coffee.

"I don't think so, actually." I told her what was going on, and she listened, her face intent. When I was done, she nodded and wrote a name and number on a piece of paper.

"Here," she said, handing it to me. "This is my therapist. She's a gift."

BUT I HAD OTHER THINGS to worry about first. We were about to embark on the big-ticket items for the house in Port Townsend, with the foundation as the biggest one.

We had known from the get-go that the current foundation was shot. During the inspection, Ron had found a three-foot-long diagonal crack in the southeast corner. He'd explained, ever optimistic, that a crack in and of itself was not a guarantee of structural demise. One that shows no sign of recent growth may, in fact, be an indicator that movement has ceased, and the gap may simply be patched—a comforting prospect. Unfortunately, this theory relates only to fissures up to a sixteenth of an inch. As the saying goes, if you can fit your checkbook inside, you might as well leave it there. Ours could have easily fit two.

There was more to it, however. Ron had dug down a bit next to the wall and discovered that we had no footings. A footing is a horizontal layer that lies below the vertical foundation walls, allowing the downward pressure to displace over a wider area. Those who have worn high heels can grasp this concept quickly. We know how it feels to take those precarious shoes off, the sudden feeling of balance and stability. A house is not that different from a human in that regard. You can stay on heels for only so long before things start to go sideways.

"Well," Ron had said, wiping his hands on his jeans, "the good thing about a new foundation is that you know what you've got."

And that was that.

AT THIS POINT, WE'D been working for months to get the house ready to be raised up for its new foundation, but I had yet to meet the man who was going to do the heavy lifting. I was beginning to wonder if his elusiveness was a bad sign, but according to the locals there was only one person for the job.

"Do you have Joe Mitchell?" everyone asked. Apparently you didn't hire Joe so much as receive him, too, like a gift.

"Why don't you come to the Baxter house with me tomorrow?" George suggested. "Joe's going to raise it. You could meet him and see how they lift a house."

So early the next morning, George and I pulled up to the Baxter house, a one-story bungalow surrounded by a meticulously land-scaped yard. Cherry trees and daffodils appeared frozen in horror at the invasion of trucks, and yet I noticed not a single broken branch, not a footprint in the flower beds, even though the trucks were huge and men with heavy boots were flowing in and out underneath the house like ants.

It wasn't until I looked in through the entry that had been cut in the old foundation that I comprehended the extent of what had already happened. Peering into the dark underbelly of the house, I could see what looked like seven-foot-tall Lincoln Log towers inter-spersed throughout the space, like toys left behind by giant children. Heavy steel beams ran from tower to tower, and then out through holes that had been cut in the sides of the house.

"Those are called cribs." George nodded in the direction of the towers. "The jacks go on top, and they raise the house."

He looked about. "There's Joe," he said, pointing over to where a tall, thin man was circling the cribs, hands in his pockets, head cocked to one side, seeming to listen as much as look. As he moved, he ducked automatically under the steel beams, bobbing up and down like a hungry heron. George called him over.

"This is your next customer," he told Joe, introducing me.

Joe grinned and shook my hand, then put his hands back in his pockets, raising his shoulders and ducking his head. He wore a green-and-turquoise fleece hat with earflaps; under his sheepskin-lined jean jacket, faded almost to white, I saw a sweatshirt that sported the saying in cartoon bubble letters I HAVE BEEN CHOSEN.

"I see you still haven't shaved," George commented.

"Oh no." Joe's eyes started dancing.

"It's a superstition," George informed me. "Don't shave until the job is done."

"Hey," said Joe, a bit defensively, "it's true. Last time I shaved, we dropped a dolly in the power ditch within the first five minutes."

He turned to me. "It wasn't a big deal, but you do have to be careful about that sort of thing." He went off to check another part of the house.

George pointed to a shiny red box the size of a steamer trunk, covered in knobs, standing near the opening to the basement. "That's a unified hydraulic jack system," he said. "Before they had those machines, they used a team of guys to raise a house, one on each jack. Raise one part of the house an inch or so, then another. It wasn't very precise, though. These machines work all the jacks at the same time and take the guesswork out of it."

"We're ready," Joe called out, and we scuttled out from underneath the house as the red machine started to growl. Neighbors and workers gathered in a circle around the machine, as if to watch the lighting of an enormous bonfire—an unsettling image.

"Okay," yelled Joe. "Go!"

At first there was only the growling noise of the machine, but then I heard a deep-seated creak and a crackling like fireworks in a far-off town. The indicator on the side of the machine slowly started to move—2, 4. The thinnest of cracks began to show between the shingles and the foundation as the structure lifted, inch by inch, making snapping noises. The meter moved up to 8, 10. The house rose, slowly, ponderously, movements so subtle they were barely visible, and yet the cumulative effect was immense. A house, tons upon tons of weight, raised by twelve jacks the size of jugs of cheap wine.

The machines stopped at fourteen inches, and the house sat perched like a Victorian lady holding up her skirts at the sight of a mouse. The men scurried in and out with more pieces of cribbing.

"It seems so strange," I said, "to see it sitting up there, unattached."

George looked over and smiled. "Well, you know most old houses aren't connected to their foundations anyway, right?"

"Wait. What?"

"New ones are bolted down, but the old ones just sit on top."

I thought of earthquakes, windstorms, floods—all things that happen in the Pacific Northwest on a fairly regular basis.

"What keeps old houses in place?" I asked.

"Gravity," George said. "And luck."

How could I not have known this? I wondered. Or maybe I did know but just didn't want to acknowledge it, the way we never really want to acknowledge the suspension of disbelief necessary to move through our daily lives—to drive large metal objects at high speeds, get married, have children. Who could ever sleep soundly knowing their house was just itching to go on a walkabout? I had a vision of our hundred-year-old Craftsman in Seattle. We'd lived there for more than a decade, and we'd never actually been safe, if you thought about it.

IT IS PROBABLY FITTING that many houses in the United States are not attached to their foundations. We are a mobile population, after all. In 2007, the US Census Bureau calculated that the average American will move 11.7 times in their life, while Europeans will move only four times on average, according to a RE/MAX Europe study.

In this way, I am a completely typical American. I grew up moving. West to east to west. North to south to north. Not every year, but every five or so—an awkward length of time. I learned early the art of the quick setting down and pulling up of roots. I made friends, and then let them go. In that pre-Facebook time, I knew those friendships would never survive a life of hand-scrawled letters.

Perhaps that's why as a general rule I remember the houses we lived in better than the people I knew. To this day, I am horrible at recognizing faces—but I can tell you the floor plan of almost any house I've ever been in. There is a mnemonic device developed by the ancient Romans called a memory palace. You take a building you know well, then mentally place each thing you want to remember within a specific room. The location helps you recall the memory. But for me, the building *is* the memory.

Ben, as you might suspect, had a different experience. He grew up in the same city for most of his life. He tends his friendships, and his network of contacts is legion. He is like one of those plants that you pull out of its pot to find there is no soil left, every bit taken up by roots. From the moment we met, I loved the centeredness of him. I wanted to be near it, and to have that for our future children. With each of their births I could feel a web forming between us. But it was when we lived in Italy that the concept of roots became a visual, tangible thing. I watched the love flowing down through the generations. You could almost taste it in the air. I wanted that for our family.

But here is where the irony of our current situation loomed large. In my desire to create a more family-oriented way of life, I was spending half my time away from my children and husband. And the stress was high enough that when something like the almost-fire happened, I saw only the risk that had come so near to our home. Just like when I was young, I kept focusing on the house, more than on the people within it. If I truly wanted a foundation for us, I knew that equation would need to change.

THE RED MACHINE GROWLED into action again, and the Baxter house raised higher. When it was finally dangling above our heads, Joe walked over.

"What do you think?" he asked me.

"Amazing."

"By the way," he said, "have you ever thought about moving your house?"

"What?"

"I mean, once it's in the air, we can do whatever you want. Forward, backward, twirl it like a top. Why not? And it won't change the cost much."

This really was the day for having my mind blown, I decided.

George leaned forward, intrigued. "Hey, that's a good idea. The north side of the house sits too close to the street anyway—if we moved the house deeper into the lot, that would help."

He was right, I realized. For the most part, the setting for our house was the feng shui definition of perfect—facing south, on a hill, looking out to water, and surrounded by greenery. The one thing that had always bothered me was how close to the road it was. With those tall walls, it felt like it was looming over the passing cars.

I'd always thought that was just one of those things you had to accept. Now, I tried to picture it—our two-story house, spinning like a ballerina, choosing its own site.

"Maybe," I said. Then, "Okay."

"Great," Joe said. "We'll get on it."

UNFORTUNATELY, HOWEVER, WE WERE having problems getting the city to approve a plan for our new foundation. It turns out the fill dirt below our house went even deeper than anyone had thought. The original concept had to be scrapped, and a new one was being devised with something called pin piles—thick pieces of galvanized metal pipe, driven down through loose soil until they strike hard dirt and stay, rock solid. The footings for the house are then attached to the pipes, the foundation walls are poured on top of the footings, and the house is, finally, bolted to the foundation.

Rumor had it that the plan for our new foundation could include as many as ninety pin piles, pounded deep into the ground. I'd said I wanted roots; it looked as if I'd get a whole metal forest of them.

The plans were not cleared through the city yet, but Joe had only the one opening in his schedule in the next four months. And so, with yet another leap of faith, we decided to lift our house—even if we didn't know what would be going underneath it.

IT WAS AN EARLY Saturday morning at the end of April when Ben, Kate, Ry, and I set out, anticipating the thrill of seeing our house rise off the ground in its own magic trick of levitation. I'd told the kids about the Baxter house, and they were both disbelieving and excited, a rare feeling of family unity in the past weeks. The traffic that morning was unusually bad, however, each stoplight turning red, the cars sauntering along. Ben switched lanes like a slalom skier trying to dodge each gate, but it barely made any difference. The minutes were ticking away, and there was nothing I could do about it. When we finally pulled up to the ferry dock, the orange-vested man directing traffic put his palm up to pause us as we reached the front of the line.

I sat in the car, fingers crossed so hard I was afraid they'd crack. The last long couple of months had been hard ones. We'd pounded and sweated and smashed. We'd breathed in odors we hadn't known existed. The week before, as I had sledgehammered my way through the very last wall of plaster, I'd encountered dead rat number twenty-eight, covered in hundreds of crawling white maggots, which simply evaporated as the light hit them.

And each time I'd left my family behind in Seattle, each time I couldn't figure out what to say to Kate or Ben, we'd grown a bit further apart, disappearing to each other. A magic trick indeed.

Through all those months, there had been a stick and a carrot motivating us: the money we needed to save by doing the demolition ourselves, and the prospect of seeing the house lifted off the ground. The latter was the payoff for all of the work, the event that could bring us all back together.

We really, really needed that carrot.

I sent the ferryman a look of desperation—*please, we must get there in time*—but when a boat is full, it is full, and thus we were stuck, first in line for the next ferry, one of the few times in life when being number one is the last thing you want to be.

THE SITE WAS LITTERED with trucks and cars when we arrived, the house up about three feet off its foundation. A metal ladder leaned precariously where the front stairs had once been. The ragged ends of the wooden supporting beams dangled in the air; where the asbestos shingles had been removed, the diagonal sheathing underneath was now exposed, black with rot. George was encircling the area with a yellow ribbon printed with CAUTION in bold black letters, which made it look as if we should have a hurricane named after us.

The kids were eagerly eyeing the ladder. At such times, they could look so much like their father it was uncanny.

"Can we go in?" they asked George.

"Sure," he said. "It's steady as a rock."

"Be careful," I said, but they were already scrambling up the rungs like sailors aiming for a crow's nest. Ben followed.

Joe came up and saw me considering the caution tape. "You don't have to worry," he said, "Nobody will go in now. Once a house goes up, they never go in."

"How much did it weigh?" I asked, hoping for good news.

"It was light. Thirty-five tons. That's good. Lighter is cheaper. You all got a lot out of there."

I started adding numbers in my head. We'd taken out seven and a half tons of trash. Ten and a half tons of plaster and lath. Seventeen tons of chimney. And then I realized something—by my calculations, we now had exactly half the house we had started out with.

"HEY, MOM," RY CALLED from the front porch, "come in and see this."

I clambered up the ladder, the metal rungs hard beneath the soles of my tennis shoes. Kate and Ben and Ry were standing by the south-facing windows looking out.

"It's like being in a tree house," Ry said, looking down at the ivy that covered the orchard. He was right. Three feet in elevation is no great distance—the height of a preschooler, the depth of the shallow end of a swimming pool—and yet the perspective was completely changed. It made flying feel possible.

I turned and gazed around at the interior. There was still more demolition to do. The old windows and all that rotten diagonal sheathing would soon be gone. We weren't keeping that much—a floor plan, a collection of studs, a memory of bones. On the north side of the living room, near the door, I spotted the outline of the old front stairway on the wall, visible now, heading up like a directional arrow. *Keep going.*

BY THE TIME WE went outside again, Joe and his crew had finished loading up their gear and were standing around swapping stories and jokes. Ben got a call and walked off down the road a bit, talking quietly into his cell phone.

"So how do you move a house?" Ry asked Joe.

"Soap," he said.

"Soap?"

"Yeah, well, I didn't get it either at first," Joe said. "I mean, flakes? Liquid? Finally, we got some guys down at the house movers' convention in Texas to tell us. They said Ivory soap, in bars. And you need it to be really fresh. Safeway goes through the most volume, so we get it there, same day we use it."

He grinned and headed off to his truck, as if his explanation made all the sense in the world.

"Soap?" Ry said to me. I just shook my head, as confused as he was.

The trucks pulled away, and the kids, seeing that the source of entertainment had left, wandered down into the lower yard to look at the cribs. The towers reminded me of the Jenga game, the one with all the blocks where you take out one at a time and hope the whole thing doesn't fall down.

"Don't go under the house," I called to the kids. They looked back at me.

"Duh," Kate said, but she smiled just a little.

AS I WATCHED THEM wandering between the ivy orchard and the house, Ben walked back up, putting his phone in his pocket.

"You remember the stock we sold to buy the house?" he said to me in a low voice.

I nodded. It was hard to forget, especially with our investment looming above us in all its questionable glory.

"The stock's gone down eighty percent in the last three months," he said.

"You're kidding."

"No," he said, shaking his head in disbelief. "We would have lost everything."

I walked straight into his arms and stayed there for a long moment. Then I went over to our foundationless house, stretched up on my toes, and kissed it.

"Thank you," I whispered.

DESIGN

It's a lot easier to correct mistakes with
an eraser than with a sledgehammer.

—George Nash

AND THEN, AFTER ALL that sweat and destruction, all those deadlines and anticipation, everything stopped while we waited for the city to approve the plan for our foundation. Week after week after week.

There are few things you can do while you're waiting for the wheel of bureaucracy to slowly crank its way around to you. Worry is one of them; design, its more logical and productive sibling. Design happens in the realm of the mind, on its own schedule. Thus, while we might not have been able to make physical progress on the house, we could at least move forward in our imaginations.

The interesting part—stuck there in the no-man's-land between reality and fantasy—was knowing that each choice we made now would influence who we would become once those plans turned into our home.

THE FIRST TIME I REMEMBER consciously thinking about how the designs of our built environments affect us was when I was a new student at Occidental College and encountered the administration building. The structure rises up in the center of the campus like

Mount Olympus itself, a giant glass cube, its four corners supported by angular white columns. The walls of the main floor are made of clear glass, through which you can see across an almost empty lobby. No desk, no receptionist, only a few tall potted plants. In the middle of the floor, a large staircase spirals down to the subterranean and often windowless lower administration offices. An elevator tucked discreetly into a wall of the main lobby whisks you to the offices of the upper administration, which seem to float above the earth, protected from view by walls of tinted glass. No matter how hard the various presidents of the college have tried to be egalitarian, open, and receptive, the very building they work in works against them.

When Winston Churchill made his famous comment about shaping our buildings, and their corresponding effect upon us, it was part of his impassioned plea to re-create the House of Commons in its original form after the bombings of World War II. Churchill prevailed, and the iconic rectangular room where the two political parties face each other was reconstructed. Through his words, Churchill helped to ensure tradition and patriotism, but he also shaped the way that the British government would function moving forward. It would take great imagination to see beyond a two-party system, given that there is literally no room for anything different.

Space matters. How we divide it matters. When architecture student Michael Murphy worked with physician Paul Farmer to develop new kinds of hospitals in Rwanda, they created buildings where the corridors are outside, air circulation is natural, and each bed has a window. Mortality rates plummeted. Later, for a completely different project in Montgomery, Alabama, Murphy designed a powerful and architecturally brilliant memorial dedicated to the African American victims of lynching and oppression. From a distance, the building is low and classical in appearance, with what looks like a series of slender supporting pillars. It is only when you enter the building that you realize that, like Eisenman's House VI, most of the pillars do not reach the ground. In the case of the memorial, however, there is a different kind of subversion at work. The pillars become a stunning visual, a forest of hanging bodies where structure should have been. The effect is chilling, felt in the gut as much as the mind.

Around the world, architects are creating buildings that interact with both humans and their environment in new and energizing ways. Ross Chapin is building pocket neighborhood communities, clusters of small houses where parking is separated from living, and owners walk along a winding path past front porches, greeting their neighbors as they go. Moshe Safdie is reinventing the concept of high-rise apartments, designing structures that have light and green space, community areas, rooftops gardens, and walkways. And Keren Brown Wilson changed the way we think of assisted living centers for the elderly, proving that autonomy and control can be their own form of medicine.

A STUDY BY THE ENVIRONMENTAL Protection Agency in 1989 determined that Americans spend more than 90 percent of their time indoors—a number that has almost certainly risen since then. This means that whatever influence our buildings have upon us, they get a lot of time to do it—even if we are not consciously aware of it. We feel it, though. We wander about a cavernous great room and find ourselves unable to settle. Other times, we walk up a wide front porch, and it is as if arms have invisibly opened to us. We make our way through a sunlit house, seemingly drawn from one room to the next. Houses embody their own kind of magic; we just rarely pay attention to the magicians.

During the years I did real estate, I would go on the company tour of new listings every Tuesday morning. It got to the point where I could tell almost without thinking which houses would be problematic to sell. Not because of a neon-orange bedroom, or the pastel-pink toilet in the bathroom, although those things never helped. This had to do with movement, feeling. Thirty agents would descend upon a home, and I would watch them make their way through it, almost like a dye test running through arteries, a living manifestation of energy moving, or not, through the house. Those houses where the agents crowded together at a tight intersection between kitchen and dining room, or spun around, looking back and forth as if they couldn't remember if they'd seen all the bedrooms—those were probably going to sit on the market for a while.

Flow is a crucial factor in a house. We are most comfortable in homes that start with welcoming entries, a feeling that continues as we move through rooms that gradually shift from public to private, each space having its own defined purpose as well as a transition to the next. This is an organizing principle we unconsciously expect, which explains our confusion when we enter a house to find a bedroom directly off the entry—it's the equivalent of having a stranger on the street suddenly turn and tell you an intimate secret. But when a house follows a recognizable organizing principle, it achieves a flow that feels natural and comfortable. We settle in.

THE FLOW OF OUR HOUSE in Port Townsend had been interrupted twice since it was built in 1909. The first occurrence was when the front staircase was removed. I'd asked around, and a neighbor told me that the previous owners had done it because they wanted more room for their Christmas tree. It seemed hard to imagine, but the staircase was definitely gone, leaving the living room tilting psychologically as well as physically.

The absence of the stairway, and the definition to the entry it had provided, also eliminated any sense of a welcome. You opened the front door into the upper quadrant of a big, impersonal rectangle of a room. It was entry as anti-invitation—something those piles of trash had reinforced but was still present now without them.

Just as importantly, the traffic patterns of the house had been radically changed, leaving a hidden set of cramped back stairs as the only access to the second story. The message embedded in the new floor plan was clear: *Keep out.* Given the reclusive nature of the previous owner, it made sense. But it wasn't doing the house any favors.

The other interruption to the flow came from us when Ben cut off the narrow kitchen and the back porch that was connected to it. He'd used a chain saw, standing high up on a ladder, and it was like watching someone slice through a very moist cake. The whole thing fell off the side of the house, landing on the ground with a wet smack. The activity was deeply satisfying, and, given the levels of rot and decomposition we'd found, it was the only thing we could have done, but it left us with a few problems. Before that point, the angular box of our Foursquare had been softened by the presence of the front and back porches, their roofs extending the gentle slope of the hipped version above. When we removed the kitchen and the back porch, however, we also destroyed the symmetry they had provided.

Nature and humans love symmetry; research suggests that evenly proportioned facial features send a message of health and good genes, and I believe that building proportions are no different. Balanced structures simply feel stronger—if you need convincing, just try to imagine the White House with only one wing. With our back porch and kitchen gone, the abruptness of the west side of our house was disconcerting. Whether inside or out, people instinctively kept looking for what wasn't there.

And then there was a second problem: we now had no kitchen.

Ben and I had played around with plans for a new kitchen in a newly built room—full of light, a place to gather—but given all the infrastructure costs we were racking up, we knew we were just fantasizing. Around and around we went, with no logical or emotionally satisfying conclusion to be found.

ENTER ROMAN.

"So, I had some ideas . . ." he said as he walked into the house for our meeting.

I was starting to understand that Roman often started discussions this way. He pulled a large roll of drawings out of his worn leather briefcase and unfurled them across our dirty but trash-free carpet. They were initial ideas at this stage, but hand drawn, precise, and elegant. A work of art.

"Walk me through it?" I asked him.

"Let's start with the living room," he said, and pointed at the drawings to a set of stairs.

Ben and I had agreed that we wanted to rebuild the front stairway—it was our one extravagance, but we believed it would make the most difference to the house. When Roman showed me the staircase on paper, it made the rightness of the decision real. The steps rose, turning at a landing at the halfway point, then disappeared like a secret invitation. They were graceful, but they also gave weight and definition to the north side of the room once again.

"I added this, too. I wanted to give you more of an entrance," Roman said, pointing to a framed opening that divided the ungainly rectangular front room into two parts: an entry with the staircase on the north side, and a living room to the south. It was strange how quickly I relaxed as I looked at the entry; I might have expected the opposite, given the square footage we were losing from the living room, but that wasn't the case. Like porches, entries are important architectural elements that subliminally affect our relationship both with a house and the people within it.

One of the things that had always been difficult about our home in Seattle was that, like many Arts and Crafts houses, the front door was centered on the house, and entering it dropped you directly into the middle of the living room. Arranging furniture was a nightmare, as was greeting or saying goodbye to guests. No one knew what to do. At the end of an evening, people would stand by the front door, sweating in their coats, circling around like flies. It was as if they didn't know how to leave. Evenings always seemed to end with a whimper, a series of less and less enthusiastic hugs, rather than the bang of a happy farewell. The house in Port Townsend had presented a similar problem, with its large amorphous living room.

But with Roman's plan, we had an entry—a place to shed your public self along with your coat and become part of the family. And there was a chance for anyone to be family, too—the open invitation in those stairs told you so.

"I love it," I said to Roman.

"The trick," he told me, "is to keep the finish work consistent." The frame that partitioned the entry and living room included half-height bookshelves on either side, each with a column rising from the top of the shelves toward the ceiling. While the main opening provided you entry to the living room, the open spaces above the bookcases offered two additional intimate views. Caught up as we usually are with exterior views, it is easy to overlook the potential of interior ones—which can be particularly important in the Northwest, where our skies can be grey and cloudy a good portion of the year.

I noticed Roman had also taken out the pocket doors that originally divided the living and dining rooms and replaced them with the same framed-opening-with-bookshelves concept. The repetition created a pattern, a visual trick that established a feeling of coherence even as it kept your eye moving forward.

Recurring elements are an especially effective way to create a sense of flow, and most houses have their own particular features. Arched doorways, double-hung windows, hefty baseboards, a geometric pattern that shows up in everything from tiles to leaded glass—each becomes part of the signature, or refrain, of the house. Noting and replicating a house's signature features can help create a seamless transition between new and old in a renovation.

While Roman's framed openings were not currently present in the house, they were completely consistent with its vintage, and their repetition created a new refrain that was then repeated throughout the main floor, tying it all together.

"Look here." Roman pointed at the plans to a set of French doors at the south end of the living room, where the chimney had once been. The glass doors were flanked on either side by the two narrow windows that had previously surrounded the fireplace.

I looked up to see how the plan would manifest in reality and saw how the blank space where the chimney had once been now framed a view of Mount Rainier, far off in the distance. It was a worthy successor to the fireplace, I had to admit.

"Keep looking," Roman said, pulling my attention back to the plans. I peered more closely, and then I saw it. The dimensions of the

French doors matched the framed openings between the main rooms, and the windows on either side echoed the spaces above the bookshelves. He'd used the same theme he'd already established, only this time he gave us the exterior view.

He smiled when he saw me catch it.

"Details," he said. "It's all in the details."

NOW IT WAS TIME FOR the tough stuff. "So what are we going to do about the kitchen?" I asked, taking a deep breath.

"I thought we'd put it here." He motioned toward the northwest corner of the house.

My breath came out in a rush. "The yuck room?" I said. What was he thinking? It was the only dark, isolated spot in a house otherwise filled with light and views. Besides—it was the yuck room.

"I spend a lot of time in the kitchen," I said. *How could he have gotten me so wrong?*

"Oh, well, we'll open it up," Roman said amiably, pointing to the plans once again.

And suddenly there it was, a wonderful square space with a large opening on the south wall, connecting it to the dining room. The opening was framed like the other two, but this time there was a kitchen bar providing a partial division, keeping the mess of the kitchen out of sight while allowing the cook full access to the view.

As I looked at the plans, I could feel all the darkness of that room fade away, and the four squares of the house fall into place with a satisfying thump. The rooms still performed the function of four strong columns—entryway, living room, dining room, and kitchen psychologically holding up the house—but the flow between them would be easy and unencumbered. In fact, the only interior door on the main floor was to the basement. And yet each room had its own character, was its own chapter in the larger story of the house.

"Wow," I said. I thought of all the hours Ben and I had spent working on the problem of the kitchen, never once reaching this simple and elegant solution.

"It just made sense," Roman said, shrugging.

The design was ingenious, but it still left a plywood wall on the west side of the house where the old kitchen had been. I glanced over; I couldn't help it. The lack of balance kept drawing my attention like a loose tooth.

Roman caught me looking. "I thought you said you couldn't afford—"

"No, you're right," I said.

Actually, with the kitchen situation solved, we no longer needed to rebuild a room there, not in any practical sense. And yet I could feel the house yearning in that direction.

Roman saw my expression.

"How about this?" he asked. "We'll go ahead and put a frame for a door inside the wall now. When you've got the money, you'll have a head start."

It reminded me of Aravena's buildings in Chile, the way the open spaces between them became a belief in the future, and in the meantime, a promise.

"Thank you," I said.

"OKAY." ROMAN RETURNED TO the plans in front of us. "Want to look at the upstairs?" He flipped to the next page. On the second floor, too, we had wanted to make some adjustments. The original bathroom had consisted of two four-foot-wide rooms centered on the south wall of the house. One slim and gloomy rectangle held a toilet, while the other contained a sink and the shower with its rubber-glove-covered handles. It wasn't just that I didn't like the idea of ever taking a shower in there; it seemed a strange use of space and a waste of a view.

But there had been another option. The northeast bedroom was the one with the least view, and it was about to lose a chunk of its space to the rebuilt stairway, anyway.

"What if we turned that bedroom into a bathroom?" I'd asked Roman, and he'd nodded thoughtfully, then played around with plumbing issues in his head until coming up with a solution that would work.

That had just left the question of what to do with the square footage where the bathroom had been. Ben and I were in favor of adding it on to the main square of the master bedroom, creating a narrower adjoining sitting area that looked out at the view. Roman had been hesitant about the idea from the very beginning, without ever saying exactly why. He'd talked about moving doors, adding partial walls, anything to juggle the shape. I could see on the plans now that he was still working with the issue. I began to wonder—as none of his suggestions were necessarily structural in nature—if perhaps there was a less scientific reason that he didn't feel comfortable talking about.

I decided to fall on my own sword.

"You know," I ventured, "I don't know much about this stuff, but I've heard that an L-shaped room is supposed to be bad feng shui." Roman was looking at me curiously, but not leaping into the conversation. I soldiered on. "I mean, apparently a room that's lacking a corner—in this case, the marriage corner—could be unpromising for a master bedroom."

He nodded. "Well, you know Port Townsend is terrible for marriages." He paused. "I probably shouldn't have said that, but it's true. You need to have a really strong marriage to live here."

I knew Roman was divorced; I wasn't sure what I should say.

"I know what I'm talking about. I have access to information." His face was serious.

Ah, I thought. *Insider architect knowledge.* Architects so often end up knowing things about their clients that they might not divulge to their best friends. What a strange and unusual situation that is.

I jumped at the chance to talk to Roman about it.

"So . . ."

"It's true," he said. "Port Townsend is actually a locus of sexual dysfunction."

I hadn't expected that. "Well," I said slowly, "it is a small town. I'm sure it feels that way." *Poor Roman*, I thought. *He must have had some incredibly difficult clients.*

"No." Roman's tone was patient. "There are forces at work. It's like how the Middle East will always be at war, because it's a locus for conflict in the world. We know this, you see, because any time an intelligent species progresses past a certain point, they are monitored."

Oh.

"I take it that it wouldn't be people doing this monitoring?" I asked.

"Oh no." He smiled. "It's nonphysically based universal entities, parts of the Universal Family."

"Now," he said, turning easily to the plans, "do you think we need two thirty-two-inch windows here? We're getting a little tight on the energy calculations."

I CALLED BEN AFTER Roman left.

"Our architect believes in aliens," I said.

He laughed—he actually laughed. "How are the plans?" he asked.

"Gorgeous. Brilliant."

"Okay then."

"But—"

"How tall are the doors?" he said.

"Standard height." This was the second conversation of the day that was not going in the direction I'd thought it would.

"Well," Ben said, and I could hear a teasing note enter his voice, "if he was really thinking about future resale, he would have made them three-feet tall, right? He designed this for us. We should consider ourselves lucky."

That is the thing about Ben. He does tend to put things in perspective.

ROOTS

A lasting architecture has to have roots.

—I. M. Pei

WE WERE WELL AND truly into summer, and we still did not have an approved foundation plan. Ben's and my original and hopelessly unrealistic schedule had us finished with the entire renovation by the end of August. It seemed likely we'd still be hanging high above the ground at that point, having lost precious months of good building weather. Ben, undaunted, used his days on-site to continue removing the rest of the heavy asbestos shingles from the now much-taller house, bringing each one down the ladder, then starting back up again, a living incarnation of Sisyphus. I loaded the shingles in the mandated hazardous-materials bags that ripped with every sharp edge. The work was ridiculously frustrating, and it terrified me to see Ben so far off the ground—but he would just say he'd rather work high now than in the rain later.

On the days when I was out there by myself, I headed to the lower garden to work on the orchard, the house dangling far above me. There is something unnerving about looking up to see your house floating above your head, like the moment in between tossing your laughing baby into the air and feeling her body in your hands once more. Neither houses nor babies are meant to fly; we know this instinctively, and yet still we send them skyward. Whether this is a sign of stupidity or faith depends, I suppose, on your ability to catch whatever falls. Those days, my confidence in both was rather shaken.

But the orchard needed help. The ivy had so completely covered the trees that it was hard sometimes to believe they were there at all. There was something almost seductive in the ivy's persistence, the wavelike feeling of all that green coming in, washing over. Standing in the orchard, it was easy to imagine that a nap taken there could last a hundred years.

IVY IS A PLANT OF opportunity, a natural invader brought to this country by settlers from Europe in the early eighteenth century. Its human history goes back all the way to the Romans and Greeks, whose poets wore it like a crown. Later, it was donned by those who believed it could help mitigate the effect of intoxication—which explains the ivy painted on signs over the doors of some English pubs. There was even a time when ivy was draped across houses and churches at Christmas, until the practice was denounced as pagan.

Perhaps it was the accumulated associations that made the plant something a settler would want to bring to a new country. Perhaps the very vibrancy of the plant was encouraging to those facing a challenging new landscape. In the end, however, ivy latched on to this new country and dug in.

In temperate climates like the Pacific Northwest, ivy has an advantage over the deciduous trees it loves to climb, as ivy is able to photosynthesize throughout the winter, gaining ground and strength every year as the trees sleep. Ivy cares almost nothing for seasons; it simply grows, as high as ninety feet, snuffing out the light necessary for the understory of forests and creating what have been termed *ivy deserts*. Although technically not a parasite—its vines do not penetrate the bark of the tree it invades—its accumulated weight can bring down a tree. Given all the assembled evidence, there is little reason to continue planting the stuff, and yet we do, watching with nostalgic awe as it climbs houses, and takes over trees.

I'VE ALWAYS DREAMED OF having an orchard—a leafy green world of reading spots and hiding places. Old orchards are best; as the trees grow toward each other, the air becomes rich with their conversations. Their branches crook and grow lichen, and yet they still bloom. I'd always said I would rather save an old orchard than plant a new one, but as I'd never owned any sort of orchard before, it made the claim easier to make. Now, I had to put my muscles where my mouth was.

Ours was not a particularly big orchard—maybe some four or five trees; it was hard to tell. Considering the density of the ivy in the lower yard, it was amazing the trees were still alive at all. The vines spread across the ground and spiraled their way up the trunks, turning the trees into burly, shaggy beasts. When the ivy reached the top branches, it stretched across the spaces toward the nearby evergreens.

You could almost hear the ivy whispering—*these trees are mine.*

The hell they are, I thought, and I grabbed the nearest vine and pulled.

ON MY DAYS BACK in Seattle, I had begun seeing the therapist my friend had recommended. The almost-fire had been a wake-up call in many ways. Up to that point, I had hoped that by simple good intentions I could let go of old ways of parenting, passed down to me through generations. I would forge a new path, allow my children to live their own lives, love them unconditionally. But it was clear that intentions were not strong enough, and so I went to Camille, a tranquil and deeply intelligent psychologist.

For fifty minutes at a time, I would sit in her office and find my way through as she listened, her mind awake, intent. Once, as a shorthand explanation of my childhood, I'd told her about my mother receiving flowers one afternoon when I was about eight years old, and my surprise when she'd said they were from my father.

"He misses me," my mother had said, and I'd asked why.

"Because he's working in DC now. He's waiting for us to sell the house and go join him," she'd replied, as if it should be obvious.

He'd been gone three months, apparently. I'd thought he was just on another business trip.

I told that to Camille as a story, a joke almost—we were still in the debriefing stage of therapy. I didn't mention my mother's reaction when she finally grasped my confusion, the mixture of shock and sadness on her face.

"That's interesting," Camille noted, "the way you told me that." And I could almost feel the tug on something deep within me, bringing it out into the light.

THERE ARE SEVERAL WAYS to get rid of ivy, none of them easy or guaranteed. Cutting the vines is to be avoided, as it can spur on additional growth. Experts suggest using herbicides, slicing into the thicker roots during the growing season and applying toxins directly into the nutritional main line. Some even recommend blowtorches. Most agree, however—the only way to gain the upper hand on ivy is to use both of your own and pull it out, year after year.

It is not a simple matter of unwinding the vines, following their sinuous trails up around the trunks and branches. Ivy latches on, using thousands of tiny hairlike suckers. When the vines are young and pliable, detaching them is a bit like removing a piece of duct tape, but as they grow and thicken, they achieve the tenacity of octopus arms. Once removed, they still leave marks behind, navigational scars for future generations—a reminder that you will be back again if you want to win this battle.

George had let me borrow Marge the dump truck yet again; I was going to have to start paying rent on the thing, he joked sometimes, but he never charged me. And a big truck was necessary—the ivy rose fifteen feet above my head, higher when it had a taller tree to climb. I worked my way up the first tree I could get to, yanking down whole sections of leaves and vines, which fell like vast green umbrellas on my head, scattering years' worth of accumulated dust. Over the hours, the tree emerged—branches reaching upward stiffly, aiming for the sky. It would take a while before they would relax; they were so used to battling for the light. When the pile behind me threatened to block my way out, I would carry great armloads to the truck, where I'd climb in and stomp them down.

By the end of the day, I had filled Marge to the brim of her wooden side panels. From my vantage point high on top of the pile, I looked back at the orchard. One small section was cleared. We had measured trash by the ton; it appeared that landscaping would be by the truck-load. Weeding on the grandest of scales.

FINALLY, IN EARLY AUGUST, the city approved our foundation. Ours would be the first house in the city to use pin piles, so green-lighting the engineering of it had taken longer, they said. Now, we just had to locate the kind of pipe they'd specified—which apparently was nowhere to be found.

In the meantime, George and his crew, frustrated by the lack of forward momentum, had taken to working on the house even though it was still sitting in the air—higher now, as Joe had raised it almost ten feet to make the future pin-pile work easier. One day, as I was down in the orchard, I heard Rourke, a big, rangy guy who was generally even-keeled, curse, long and loud. I looked up and saw him standing under the southeast corner of the house, a two-by-six held vertically in his hands.

"Sorry," he said when he saw me.

"What is it?"

He pointed up at the house hovering over us, at the area we'd come to refer to as Trouble Central. That was where the downspout went missing, the corner with the chimney with no footing as well as the biggest of the foundation cracks. Our own little vipers' nest of problems.

Jim, a sweet man who tended to play jazz radio on the site, was up the ladder above both of our heads. As I looked closer, it appeared they were trying to prop the house up from below with the two-by-six.

I raised my eyebrows in question.

"We started to take out that southeast window," Rourke explained.

"And the whole house started to sink," Jim added.

"About three-quarters of an inch," Rourke said, sounding impressed.

"Wait, the window frame was holding up that corner?" I asked.

"Yeah," he said. "Never seen that before."

The hole where the chimney used to be now gave a good view of the supporting beam, which looked distinctly like a sponge.

"Don't worry," Jim said, angling the two-by-six into place while Rourke cranked on the jack below it. As the pressure on the jack began to rise, I heard cracking noises.

"It'll be fine," Rourke called out. "Just wait until you see it with clean wood." He paused. "You weren't thinking of working inside the house today, were you?"

I fled to the garden.

SLOWLY, OVER THE WEEKS, the orchard emerged: three cherry trees, an apple, and a plum, as well as a bank of lilacs, which had been twisted into sculptural shapes by the accumulated weight of the ivy. There were times when I was oddly grateful for the ivy's age. In places, its branches were as thick as my arm, and I climbed them to get to the upper reaches, making the ivy an accomplice in its own destruction— an irony I relished by that point.

And still we waited for the pipe.

One afternoon in late August, as I was finally getting the upper hand on the ivy, I noticed what appeared to be the knobby black twigs of another apple tree, just visible at eye height through a rampantly tall wall of blackberries at the far end of the orchard. The blackberries were so thick I had ignored them, finding even ivy to be a more plausible opponent. Now I looked closer. It seemed impossible that a whole tree was in there—it would have been easier to hide an elephant. Intrigued, however, I began hacking my way in.

They didn't go down easy, those blackberries, scratching at my face, untying my shoelaces with their thorny vines, clinging to my legs in one last gasp of revenge, but inch by inch, I made progress.

Four feet off to my right, I spied the round green curve of an apple. I kept slashing away, revealing more and more tree branches. When I stopped—*finished* would in no way be the right word in this case—my arms were tattooed, my hair wild. The area around me looked like the aftermath of a giant catfight. But through the space I'd cleared in the blackberries, I could discern the outline of not one or two, but six additional apple trees. A whole world we hadn't known existed.

"TELL ME MORE ABOUT your father," my therapist, Camille, said one day as I sat in her office.

When I was young, I wasn't sure what to think of my father. He could lecture for hours at the dinner table on the intricacies of rocket science, or sit at the piano in our living room, the notes rolling out of him—songs that he'd written for each of us when we were born. But in everyday life, he didn't say much, liked quiet. Liked order. If, in the mad dash of childhood, you disrupted that order, he would say your name, just once, but the shortness of it always made me stop in my tracks, alert as a hunting dog. There was so much waiting there behind the three syllables of my name. I didn't understand what I had done that could generate that much emotion, held in so tight.

I was in my late thirties when my mother told me that she and my father had watched *The Prince of Tides* and he had broken down, told her that his mother used to beat him when he was a child. My parents had been married for more than four decades at that point, and he'd never said a thing. Although perhaps we might have suspected if we'd known how to look.

I remember so many things from that moment when my mother told me. The deep and utter sadness I felt for my father. The sudden clarity of understanding. The realization that all those years the thing he'd been fighting when he said my name was not *me*. He was fighting not to do what had been done to him.

THE ORDER FOR THE pipe was lost not once, but twice, and when the pipe was finally in the ground—pounded in so deep we joked you could hear people speaking Chinese through it—it still was not right. The inspector came out and insisted that it pass a particular test: one man leaning on a ninety-pound jackhammer should move a pipe no more than one inch in sixty seconds. If that seems impossible to you, you'd be right. Most of them failed the test, sinking down deeper into the fill dirt.

"This is crazy," George said after the inspector had left. "I tested those pipes with the Bobcat at ten thousand pounds per pipe—that's three times the tolerance we need. Now the city wants something different." He paced the site.

But the engineering inspection is a fact of life, much like catching a ferry or parenting. When you fail, you fail. You have no choice but to try again.

A FEW DAYS LATER, I arrived at the site to the ear-pounding sound of the air compressor. Down in the shadows between the cribs, I could see George and Rourke gripping a bucking red jackhammer, half the size of either one of them. Rourke had both hands on the handles and was pushing hard; George bore down on the base of the jackhammer with his foot. The jackhammer fought them, jerking back and forth like a giant swordfish.

The pipe under the jackhammer seemed not to be moving at all, despite the force being exerted upon it—thirty seconds, forty-five. Then just before sixty seconds, it sank smoothly and rapidly into the ground, as if it were being eaten by the earth. When the top of the pipe reached ground level, Rourke turned the jackhammer off. George looked up and saw me, and then shook his head.

They added a connector, more pipe, and then the whole process began again. Every once in a while, a pipe held—and stayed. At that, George yanked up the jackhammer and moved on to the next pipe. In one corner, Jim cut new lengths of pipe on a steel chop saw, orange sparks flying out near the rim of his round straw hat. It looked like our own little Dante's inferno down there.

After a while, they took a break. George walked over to me. His face was sweating and red; his eyes looked tired.

"We're almost done," he said. "We got in sixty-five yesterday."

It had taken fifteen minutes to put in one pipe. Sixty-five in a day seemed like a feat truly worthy of Mike Mulligan.

"This is nuts," I said. And then, "How deep do property rights go, anyway?"

"I think you're talking mineral rights at this point," said George. But he smiled when he said it, which I found just short of miraculous. Then he went back, picked up a new pipe, and turned on the jackhammer again.

BY THE END OF AUGUST, Camille and I had made some progress. I was learning to acknowledge and say what I thought, at least occasionally. One morning, we circled back to the almost-fire one more time.

"The Seattle house was your safe place," she said, holding my gaze with her own. "Now, you have to make one inside yourself. That's how we grow up."

IT WAS ALMOST SEPTEMBER by the time the pipes were set and the crew was ready to move the house into its new position. On the day of the event, Ben was out of town and Kate, already deep in antici-pation of her eighth-grade year, had decided to spend the day with a friend. She and I were finding our way back to each other, but slowly, one gesture or word at a time—an offer to help cook, a moment of respect—so I had let her make the decision for herself. Ry was excited at the prospect of moving a house, however, and thus he and I set off early that morning. No chance of missing the ferry this time.

The idea that our house might be transported by something as clean as Ivory soap came close to perfect irony. The removal of the asbestos shingles had left the house looking like a mangy cat, and what grass there was in the front yard had been tilled under by the repeated trips of the Bobcat, carrying out loads of old concrete and dirt. Dust swirled up in the gusts of wind, coating the fronds of the beleaguered palm trees. A day on the site left your skin parched, your hair stiff.

There was a regular truck convention in front of the house when Ry and I arrived. Men were moving about the site, intent upon their work. Not wanting to disturb them, we walked around the side of the house, looking for clues as to how it would all work. A few feet beyond the southern edge of the house, we discovered a new row of cribs made of freshly cut lumber. A series of heavy steel beams extended out from under the house to rest on top of the new cribs. The house hung in the air, waiting.

I pointed to the new beams. "I think the house will slide across on those," I said, "and end up on the new cribs."

Joe moved into position on a beam above us and started scrubbing it like a tanner working a skin, long strokes up and down. We saw something white in his hand.

"Is that the soap?" Ry asked.

"Yeah," Joe called down. "It helps the house move. It'll glide right along."

I must have looked concerned.

"We stop the soap a few feet from the end, though," he added.

"Why?" Ry asked.

"Well, that way, if the house starts to go too far, the friction will keep it from sliding off the end." Joe grinned.

He wasn't leaving much room for error, I noticed. I pictured the house, starting to move after so many years of being locked in place, building up momentum, flying off the ends of the beams and over the tops of the fruit trees below.

"Don't worry—it's never happened yet," Joe said.

I wanted to believe him, but in a contest between a thirty-five-ton house and three feet of friction, I had my own ideas of which might win.

AS WE GOT CLOSER to moving time, a crowd started to assemble—George and his crew, as well as the usual assortment of neighbors and townsfolk.

"Don't you just love physics?" Roman had walked up, holding a camera. "By the way, you'll get the best view from the side," he advised.

A truck motor started, and the crowd shifted in anticipation.

Ry and I walked out into the street, where we could see Joe maneuvering his shiny white pickup truck until it was poised to ram nose-first into the north wall. Then he pulled a long cable from the winch under the front bumper of the truck and quickly ran it back and forth between the truck, a Bobcat on the south side, and the house. A cat's cradle of cable. At last, he got back in the truck and revved the motor twice. After that, all I heard was the whirring of the winch. I waited but saw nothing.

"Look!" Ry said after a moment, pointing at the house. "It's moving!"

I stared. I couldn't see a thing. Or hear it, for that matter. If it was moving, where was the crackling and creaking, the moaning of the house?

"Look at the south edge of the house, Mom," Ry said. "See?"

Suddenly, I did. Slowly, gracefully, the house was moving toward the orchard, traveling by us like some huge decrepit Rose Parade float.

"It's hit the soap!" George called out. "Now it'll speed up."

Then the house simply slid along the beams—as if all that weight meant nothing, a shrug of the shoulders, a toss of the head.

The house maintained its stately progress, but in the process, something extraordinary began to happen. As the distance between the house and the road increased, the house shed its ominous, looming appearance. It continued to move, slower now, the friction finally kicking in, its southern corners nestling into the spreading branches of a pair of huge English walnut trees, as if they had been planted for that very purpose.

The movement stopped, and the house settled into its new home. I couldn't stop looking. In the space of five minutes, with a distance of six feet, the house had gained a new personality, a sense of belonging that had never been apparent before. I remembered Herzog's theory of how beauty could give a building *firmitas*. Maybe moving a building through the air could give it roots.

"She's wonderful," I said.

THE KITCHEN

Good buildings don't just fulfill existing
functions, they suggest new ones.
—Witold Rybczynski

ONCE THE HOUSE WAS finally on firm ground again, George's crew moved in with purpose. They had been waiting more than four months as the foundation process had dragged its way through the best weather of summer. They'd worked on the house like a high-wire act and jackhammered pipe until I worried about their teeth falling out. Now, they were in known territory again, and you could feel their pent-up energy finally gaining a purpose. The house seemed to mirror it, as if having gained a new perspective, it was ready to become its true self.

I arrived one morning to find the crew in full wrecking mode, facing the wall between the dining room and the yuck room.

"Ready?" they asked, grinning. They raised their sledgehammers and the wall came down, opening the new kitchen to the rest of the house. It was about time, in more ways than one.

ROWAN MOORE ONCE WROTE, "The placing of the kitchen in a house expresses the relative status of whoever cooks to whoever eats," and I sometimes think it would be possible to encapsulate the history of a woman's role in society simply through observing the changing architecture of our kitchens. It's a chicken-and-egg kind of thing, but what is clear is that while sometimes we have shaped our kitchens, they have always shaped us.

In early rural America, a woman's role was as a vital member of a family team. Her work was rigorous and backbreaking, the vast majority of it done in the big room that typically made up the main floor of the house. That room was also where everyone gathered, particularly in the evenings, when meals were eaten by the warmth and light of the hearth, and family members sewed, read, and talked.

Increasing affluence and technological advances changed this dynamic, but, as with the invention of the chimney, often in ways that weren't anticipated. As houses became bigger, the main floor was separated into several rooms with different functions. The parlor became a place for socializing, while the kitchen was known as the "keeping room"—an apt term, as the women who were once at its center were increasingly marginalized. This trend was only magnified with the invention of the cookstove, which allowed kitchens to be banished to basements, particularly in the city. More and more, domestic labor was being done in isolation.

It wasn't until the late 1800s that domestic advocates, such as Catharine Beecher and Harriet Beecher Stowe, began adding a layer of professionalism to the job. They advocated returning the kitchen to the main floor, and introduced the concept of workstations that organized the room around the various tasks of cooking. To us, this might sound like common sense, but it was revolutionary at the time. Even more revolutionary was the concept of designing a kitchen around the needs of the woman within it.

Electricity was introduced into many US homes in the 1920s, making housework easier, and allowing more women the opportunity to venture out into the larger world. Coincidentally—or perhaps not— it was at this same time that the commonly used term *housekeeper* morphed into *housewife*. The shift was subtle, but the change in connotation was profound: a woman no longer managed her home; she was married to it. And while a *keeper* could, theoretically, be of either gender, a *wife* is always female. Words are like linguistic rooms to hold meaning, and, not unlike architecture, they can shape expectations. This one did its work.

World War II provided a short detour for cultural norms as women were welcomed into the workforce. But when the men came home, it was back into the kitchen for the women—and then into further sequestration, in the "safety" of the suburbs. Neither women nor kitchens were to stay contained, however. Change was coming fast. In 1948, the McDonald brothers opened their first fast-food hamburger restaurant, and the floodgates were opened. And then, of course, there was television. By 1960, there was a TV set in nine out of ten households in the United States, and with their screens came a constant stream of images that alternately supported or questioned the status quo. In 1963, Betty Friedan's *The Feminine Mystique* was published, and the first countertop microwave oven came hot on its heels, in 1967.

By the 1980s, remodels and new house construction began including kitchens that were open to dining rooms or family rooms. You can point to televisions or feminism or suburbs as the likely causes for this architectural phenomenon, but the irony lies in the fact that with its more communal layout, the kitchen returned to its roots as one room for all. What was old was new again. Whether we approach this shift as a restoration or a renovation is up to us.

The one thing that has stayed remarkably consistent throughout the history of kitchens in the United States, however, is which gender works in them. While there was a significant change between 1965 and 1985 in the ratio of how much time women spent cooking compared to men—a drop from 14.1 times as much to 3.5—there hasn't been nearly the same progress since. Between 1985 and 2012, that number dropped only to 2.4, and it has shown remarkably little change since. The kitchen may have gotten nicer, bigger, and more open, but as a general rule, it is still twice as much a woman's domain.

BEFORE BEN AND I started work on the house, our ratio was even more skewed than the national average. In the name of efficiency, and without the slightest sense of irony, we had always divided our domestic roles along the lines of what we already did best. Ben did home repairs and earned a living. I cooked and managed the house and took care of the kids. To be fair, we were really, really good at our jobs, and it did save us time—but the difference between *routine* and *rut* is not that many letters.

The house project had been our chance to alter all that, and changes were happening. Given a kitchen without a wife in it, Ben was starting to cook. Out in Port Townsend without Ben to assist me, I was developing confidence in my muscles and opinions. Ben and I were both better at our new roles than we might ever have predicted, and it didn't hurt the kids to see that. I wanted our new kitchen to be emblematic of that shift, a room that invited transformation.

MY RELATIONSHIP WITH COOKING had already gone through several changes over the years. I grew up with recipes—step-by-step directions that promised, but did not guarantee, success. Ben has been known to point out that in my family we like to be right, but most importantly, we don't want to be wrong. As far as I was concerned, new recipes were a chance for failure, and, as a result, I stuck to a comfortable few.

When Ben and I moved in together, I was introduced to a more freewheeling approach to cooking. We were young and short on money, but that didn't stop Ben's creativity. He was capable of putting Worcestershire sauce and peaches on a frozen pizza, or adding just about anything in the refrigerator to Top Ramen. I watched him in horror. It wasn't the food itself, which was often inspired, actually. It was the risk of it. The chance for disaster. In any case, when he got a full-time job, I quickly kicked him out of the kitchen.

It wasn't until we moved to Italy that everything changed for me. I remember the first time I went to the vegetable vendor, an old man who owned a small stand not far from our apartment. I told him I wanted to make minestrone soup and asked him which ingredients I should use. He looked at me with that indulgent but slightly mystified expression Italians often give Americans, then opened his arms to encompass the multitudes of his stall and said: "Whatever you want."

That single sentence stunned me. I was thirty-eight years old and had no idea of what to do with such culinary freedom. I fled that day, but when I was given the opportunity to take cooking classes taught by an Italian matron, I leapt at the chance. For Ernesta, cooking was a full-body event. It involved hands, not measuring cups. Ears, not recipes. When forced, she would grudgingly write down instructions for her students, but always in Italian and using European measurements. I quickly realized that it was simpler to try and intuit what she was saying, and then it just became easier to do what she was doing.

Over time, I learned the weight of flour. The smell of just enough sage or salt. The sound of risotto when the grains of rice give that gentle gasp for more broth. I started to think of ingredients as personalities, and to daydream about which ones would want to be together, which ones could make a child's rough day better or make my husband smile. Cooking this way felt like poetry, not rules. Relationships, not order. It was a language I could speak.

When we returned to Seattle, it was also a language I could use to lure my children out of their rooms. It had power. I loved teaching it to my children, but, to be honest, I guarded it jealously from Ben. We'd left Italy, a place which celebrated motherhood, and had moved back to a country where stay-at-home mothers were disregarded at best. The reentry was hard for me. Cooking gave me an identity in the way Ben's job gave him his. I didn't want to share.

And yet when we invited people over for dinner, I would always end up incredibly frustrated. Ben would be out in the main part of the house, telling jokes and making sure everyone was having a good time. I was in the kitchen, where I wanted to be—unless, of course, it was where I was expected to be. By the time the food was ready, I was no fun to be around.

Once a year, generally in January when the weeks were long and wet and dark, Ben and I would have our annual argument, and the topic was always the same—I wanted a more equal division of labor in our household. It got to the point where the fight even had its own name: Party Boy and Kitchen Girl.

But the reality was I couldn't have it both ways. If I wanted Ben in the kitchen, I had to let him in, Worcestershire sauce and all. We would have to give up efficiency and continue to step outside of our long-standing roles even after the renovation was complete. In the blank slate of the kitchen in Port Townsend, we had a chance to design a room that could encourage us both to do just that.

WE KNEW WHAT WE wanted: a kitchen that was as honest and straightforward as the rest of the house, with an openness that continued the feeling of an ongoing conversation between a sequence of rooms. I had been reading Sarah Susanka's *Creating the Not So Big House*, and Ben and I agreed that it made more sense to have a single eating area, rather than a casual one in the kitchen and a formal dining table in its own rarely used room. Roman's idea of opening the new kitchen to the dining room would soften the formality of the latter, making it a place that served equally well for morning coffee or a full-family dinner. In addition, by eliminating the need for a kitchen table, we would gain space for more people to cook. An efficient solution, but one that would invite change.

I had told Roman that my ultimate goal was for what I called a "four-butt kitchen," with space for four people to cook without banging into one another. I wanted to use the Beecher sisters' concept of workstations, and line the walls with cabinets, each area with its own function. Bucking popular trends, Ben and I had opted not to have an island in the kitchen, as it would complicate traffic flow. Butts would bang.

In keeping with our commitment to put infrastructure first and add frills later, we agreed to keep the focus functional and child friendly. The countertops would be laminate—that workhorse of surfaces, a cheap and durable option that forgives knives, spills, and most heat. The appliances would be basic—white, not stainless, affordable and, again, forgiving. They'd be easy to clean off, which meant I would not constantly be following my family around, wiping off the fingerprints that stainless seems to attract like ants on sugar. We told ourselves we could always upgrade later, but for now the practical option also allowed for more experimentation with less stress. If we wanted to change the dynamic in our kitchen, things were going to get messy.

There was only one problem with the plan: to achieve that kitchen, we needed just a bit more room than we had. And this is where architects earn their keep. When faced with our desire for a larger space, Roman had another ingenious idea—take out the servants' stairway and give that extra footage to the kitchen, enlarging it to 11'4" × 11'4". A perfect square for our Foursquare house.

REMOVING THE BACK STAIRCASE would be an unequivocal foray into remodeling—and it would mean I'd have to give up my holier-than-thou attitude regarding the former owner's decision to take out the front stairs. But I liked the idea of the additional space for the kitchen, as well as the message the new configuration would send. In Roman's vision, the house would once more be a one-staircase home, but this time with a front stairway that offered transparency and welcome, rather than the connotations of class division and secrecy. If we were opting to use a wrecking bar, it was to create a new, and I hoped better, way of seeing the world. Not to mention a kick-ass kitchen.

Still, I paused in the decision, thinking about those back stairs and all the memories they held, even for us. We had done our hardest work using those steps, as servants of the house. I knew their every tread, every dip. Already, they were part of my body's memory.

And every time I walked by the base of those stairs, I remembered the last day of the trash clean-out, when I'd looked up and seen Ben standing on the landing, a broom in his hand. The way the sun had poured down those stairs later, and the house had seemed to breathe. The lesson my husband and the house had taught me that day. I worried about what would happen to my memories, those lessons, if the staircase was gone.

Roman pointed out that there was a second and unexpected benefit to removing the back stairs, however. Not only would we have the extra space for the kitchen, we would gain a bonus area at the midway landing, where the two staircases originally met.

"What about a closet?" he suggested. I nodded. We were short on storage space, after all.

But then Roman's face lit with a sudden excitement.

"What about a reading nook?" he asked, and then I could see it—children, and grandchildren, snuggled up in a spot halfway up the stairs, just like Christopher Robin. A nest for the imagination. It was a gift, when I had been hoping only for a justification. And it would be exactly in the spot on the landing where Ben had been standing that last day of the trash clean-out.

SOMETIMES TO CHANGE A culture, we have to build a new room or invent a word for a feeling that has not yet been defined. The Japanese have a term called *shibui*. There is no equivalent in English, but it comes with the connotations of simplicity and unobtrusive beauty. As Sarah Susanka explains, "*Shibui* often seems to arise when an architect is striving to meet a particular design challenge. When you stop to think back on houses that have made an impact on you, they'll often be the ones where an awkward problem has been cleverly solved in a way that makes you think, *Well, of course! How else could it be?*"

Those are some of my favorite moments in houses—when you come across the simple, ingenious solution, the thing that sets a house apart or offers you a new way to view your life. In our case, through Roman's imagination, what had started out as a land grab for extra space for the kitchen ended up quite differently. We got a bigger kitchen to help us change our ways, but we also got a moment of whimsy and quiet on the landing—a place to stop for a moment, listening to people talking in that communal space below, and remember a man with a broom, and the grace that can come with occasional inefficiency.

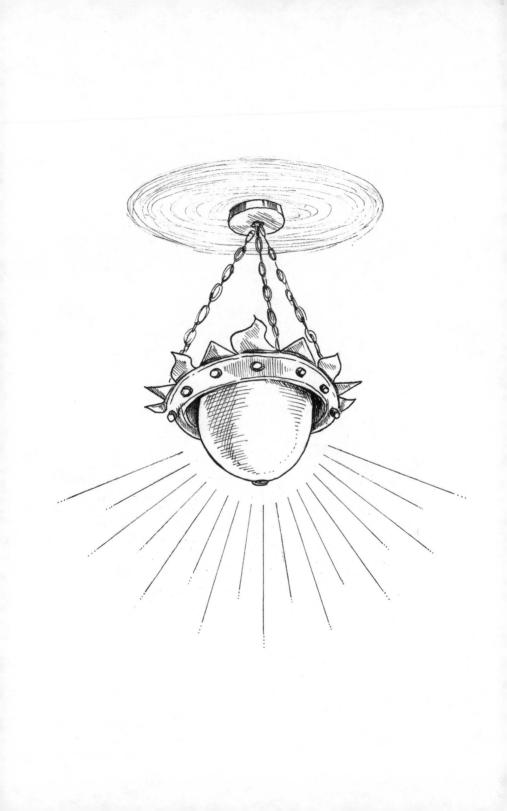

DETAILS

The most beautiful house in the world
is the one that you build for yourself.
—Witold Rybczynski

THE WINDOWS WERE CHANGING position—not much, just a touch in either direction to accommodate the restructuring of a room or two. Roman had been adamant that we alter the exterior of the house as little as possible, and thus the windows had tiptoed carefully across the plans, and I'd barely seen the change on the paper. Now George's crew removed the original wind-battered windows and marked them for disposal. Fresh two-by-fours, almost white against the darkened old studs, created a series of clean rectangles for the new windows.

I hadn't thought it would make much difference—six inches, four—and yet my view of the world outside changed with the new openings. A tree I hadn't noticed before suddenly made itself known. A stately Victorian house a quarter mile away caught my eye. For years, Ben, an avid photographer, had talked about the placement of the subject in a picture—but it was not until I looked through the new window openings that I understood how fully a small shift can alter our perception.

Back at the turn of the twentieth century, when houses such as ours were built, windows tended to be smaller, for a variety of reasons. Among them were the issues of heat loss in what were mostly uninsulated dwellings and the cost of precious glass. But Roman had explained that there was another, aesthetic reason that had its grounding in subtlety—a window seen as a frame that suggested a beauty only partially captured, leading thoughts further than the eye. Tantalizing as a path in the woods, its end around a corner, unseen.

We have less interest in subtlety these days. We want our views unobstructed, with walls of windows to let in the sky. It seems forthright and daring, an unencumbered interaction. But there is something about cutting into a building, altering any of its shapes, that makes you stop and think about what you are doing. Carpenters have a saying: "Measure twice, cut once," because once the saw enters the wood, you cannot undo what you have done. And so I found myself wondering if perhaps in our American quest to have that bigger window, we were losing the patience for tantalization, for details. A suggestion of beauty needs time to unravel and imagination to wander in. Our lives may have less time for such ramblings, but I still believe the desire for them remains.

MY LIFE HAD BECOME full of details in those days. The crew was doing infrastructure work—plumbing, framing. What they needed from me was decisions. There were choices to be made on everything from tile to carpet, cabinet styles and configurations, drawer pulls, doorknobs, sinks, faucets, appliances, vent hoods, countertops, backsplashes, toilets, tubs, towel bars, and paint colors. I was becoming the queen of *Consumer Reports*, and I spent entire days in the showrooms and discount building-supply outlets tucked deep in the industrial parks south of downtown Seattle.

If you have the money, you can turn all those decisions over to a designer, but I wouldn't have wanted to anyway. For me, a house comes alive in its details. The matching of trim work from one room to the next, the unexpected pleasure of a faucet handle that feels like water itself in your hand—the extra effort creates a sense of a life well lived and a house well loved.

That care in the details was one of the things I'd admired most about Italy. While we were living in Bergamo, workers had dug up one of the main streets in the ancient upper town, in order to do some sewer repairs. It took almost the entire two years we were there, as they painstakingly removed and then later replaced the cobblestones in their intricate fan-shaped pattern. Swapping them with asphalt would have been much easier and faster, and certainly less wear and tear on the cars that would travel across it. But while there was grumbling about the congestion the roadwork created, there was never a question of doing it differently. I still remember the day the street was finished, looking down that expanse of undulating stones, the grace of it, like a river made of rock.

It was something I mourned when we returned to our native country. While I love the American drive to get things done, I deeply missed the other—the slow slip of an artful detail into my consciousness, the softening of my soul that happened at the sight of a curve in a stone wall when a straight line would have done. I wanted to give that kind of attention to my house. I'm sure there were times when all my research and trips to one store after another seemed obsessive—and yet to me what I was doing was no different than a carpenter sanding down a piece of wood until it shines, or a writer editing a sentence until it sings. There is beauty in seeing the small things, in taking care of something. I've always thought that phrasing odd—*taking* care. I've always thought it should be *giving*.

IN FRANCE, THERE IS a small group of master craftsmen who are called *compagnons*, a tradition that dates back to the Middle Ages. *Compagnons*—or companions—spend a minimum of five years learning their craft, traveling from town to town to work under different experts.

At the end of the training, each *compagnon* must create a masterpiece that displays their talents. The tradition among woodworkers is to create a fabulously detailed miniature staircase, only inches tall. It is painstaking, precise work, and the result is a piece that is breathtaking, fit for fairies. And yet those tiny staircases provide a function for us, as well. They are proof of what we humans are capable of when we choose to love right down to the smallest details.

IN MANY WAYS, MY MOTHER instilled that passion for details in me. She was an art major in college, and a fashion designer before she had children. I still have a memory of being some five years old, twirling about the living room in one of the cocktail dresses she'd designed, its blue scalloped edges floating about my feet, every stitch flawless.

She could orchestrate the schedules of five children without getting a run in her stockings, lead a Girl Scout troop, bake cakes for every birthday, and decorate the dining room with streamers and balloons—all while keeping our house meticulously clean. She's the one that taught me to use a toothbrush to clean the grout between tiles, and to check with a glove for dust on a baseboard. She would have made an incredible project manager.

But there are downsides to having a detail-oriented parent, as my own kids would tell you. There are positive details and negative ones, and my mother could correct you five different ways during a task as simple as making coffee. I don't believe she even knew she was doing it, but it happened all the same.

She was a woman of her time, her wellspring of creativity and intelligence rerouted into the river of motherhood. She climbed over its banks the moment her children were deemed grown-up enough, getting a master's degree and then working in art museums, where she organized shows and sent the best thank-you notes anyone ever received. She loved us, but you could see what working gave her: the excitement, the stimulation, that free-ranging feeling, powerful and clean. There was a time when I begrudged it—not the work, but the joy, and the fact that it didn't come from us—until I was a stay-at-home mother and understood that desire myself, saw my own childhood expression on my children's faces, looking up at me.

So many of us declare that we will not become our parents. But they are the house we are born into. Their lives, their rules, their loves are the walls that surround us, make us. No matter what, we will always be renovations, never a clean slate. The trick, as with any renovation, is keeping the good bones.

And so I take my love of good details from my mother. When I held the schedules of plumbers and framers and roofers and finances in my brain, I felt as if I could conquer the world. When I found the blue and green glass trim tiles that would add some creativity to classic white four-by-fours while still staying in my budget, I experienced a rush of joy. And as I worked on the house in Port Townsend, I finally began to understand my mother's quest for the perfect Christmas tree—the desire to find art in the everyday, when everyday is the palette you were given.

OVER THE NEXT FEW WEEKS, I spent my time ticking off the items on my list, while the guys banged away on the house. It took time, but bit by bit I made my way through, until finally lighting was all that was left. It wasn't coincidental—lighting is either boringly simple or notoriously tricky, particularly in the Pacific Northwest, where illumination is a precious commodity during our long, dark winters. Out here, we depend upon our electric lights psychologically as well as physically, and in the dim half of the year I would go from one to the next in our Seattle house like a child leaping from rock to rock to get across a river.

Years before we found the house in Port Townsend, I had bought a new ceiling light for our dining room in Seattle. The fixture was a fanciful thing, a globe that hung down from a crown of bronze sun rays that encircled it. It didn't belong in that house; those Craftsman bungalows have their own style. But I wanted to put my mark on the dark wood-paneled room; I wanted to bring in the sun. It didn't work. The globe was thick, and the light it emitted was a mere glow when a more thorough illumination was needed. But the fixture had stayed up there on the ceiling in all its irony because I couldn't bear to take it down.

My first decision in choosing the lighting for the house in Port Townsend was to bring in that fixture, so it could go where it belonged, in a bright and open dining room. Looking out at the water and sky, it would be a partner to the real sun, not an unsuccessful act of defiance. And in the evenings, its glow, augmented by candles, would encourage long, slow dinners.

That just left some twenty-five other fixtures to find. With our budget at the screaming point, I decided to go simple and consistent with the bedrooms—choosing basic ceiling lights that matched the era. But when it came to the living room, I was stumped. In that most public room of the house, I wanted something special, something that sent a message the way the sun fixture did.

One Thursday morning in early September, I went to my local lighting store in Seattle. Only a few weeks before, standing on the same sidewalk on a hot and cloudless summer afternoon, I could not make myself go in and consider a future need for artificial illumination. But on that Thursday, the weather had turned cold and soggy, and the radiance of the store had an almost magnetic attraction. I walked inside among the ceiling fixtures, looking up.

When lights are turned off, the variation among the types of glass tends to blur to a fairly homogenous white, and the glass can take a poor back seat to the charms of the metal components, fashioned in Arts and Crafts perpendiculars or spiraling ironworked leaf and flower constructions. The metal shapes evoke cultural memories, of Versailles, Williamsburg, turn-of-the-century New York—a panorama of history hung from the ceiling of a store. It is easy to become lost among them, and the glass can become overlooked.

But when you turn a light on, everything is different. There are subtleties and surprises that have been waiting in the dark. A plain fixture can change personality when illuminated—become a gift or a private joke released only by the interplay between light and glass. It takes an agile mind to match glass to metal in a way that causes them to enhance each other. Each combination is different, and so I stood in the store and pulled the dangling chains on and off.

A half hour later, I had illuminated some fifty different fixtures. None of them seemed right. I told myself I would try one more, and then I would stop for the day. The fixture above me was not flashy or ornate, with just a delicately carved dark brown knob at the bottom that looked more like wood than metal. The knob held in place a seemingly opaque glass bell that curved outward toward the ceiling, then flared like a skirt. I almost didn't turn the fixture on—it seemed too ordinary to waste my last attempt on—but then something made me tug on the chain.

The light glowed, and the sight made my breath catch. There were clouds in the glass, swirling up the sides and then out to the edges. Light danced behind and between them. It was ethereal, balletic, movement and light and warmth all at the same time.

Seeing it took my mind back to a wet November morning in Italy. On that day, I'd been walking through the old upper town, the cobblestones damp and cold beneath my feet. When I'd entered the piazza, I saw a strange sight—a couple ballroom dancing in elegant clothes, oddly elevated above a crowd of people. The couple was not tall or on a stage, I realized; they were on stilts. He was in a black tuxedo with elongated tails, she in a long white dress with a skirt that flowed about her like a cloud. Back and forth they moved, apart from each other, then together, around and around in circles. Then he lifted her up over his shoulder, the stilts and the cloud skirt following after. A moment later, she was down again, and the music filled the air like movement itself.

Who were they? Why were they there, dancing on stilts, on stones? It didn't matter. They were magic, a moment of unexpected beauty on a dark day.

THE OWNER OF THE LIGHT STORE came up next to me. "I was wondering if you'd end up with that one," he said, smiling. "That's one of my favorites. It comes from France."

I imagined it in the living room in Port Townsend, hanging from the ceiling above the windows that looked out to the sky and the water. I was willing to throw the rest of our lighting budget into the bargain-warehouse category to get this one light. But the store owner smiled again.

"I'll give you the builder's discount," he said. "You look like you'll take good care of it."

I paid him, and he put the fixture in a box, where it lay, quiet and still. Once the drywall was in, we would hang it in the living room. It would be the clouds to the sun of the dining room fixture. A conversation between weather patterns. A dance on the ceiling above our heads.

As I walked to the car, I found myself wondering if anyone besides me would ever notice that light fixture on my living room ceiling. My guess was that most people would not—but I was willing to bet they'd feel it, all the same.

When I was in real estate, there were what I called "emotional houses," the kind that could inspire bidding wars even in the slowest of economies. As far as I could tell, it was never a house's perfection or trendiness that brought out such enthusiasm. Instead it was a quality I could describe only as an unexpected generosity, that love of a house that goes right down to the details. There is an intimacy to this kind of caretaking. It is not necessary. It is not pragmatic. But when we are near it, it creates a desire to reach beyond stability, and utility, to *venustas*—a beauty that draws us in and makes us want to stay.

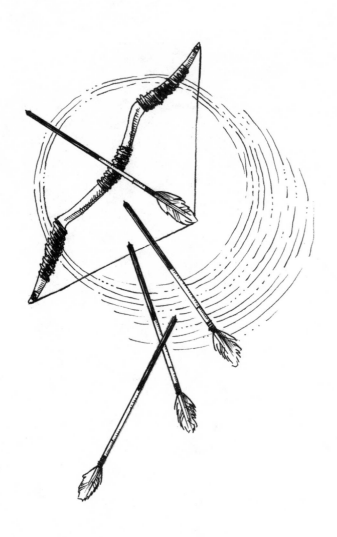

THE ROOF

*Why are we so vulnerable, so
inconveniently vulnerable, to what
the places we inhabit are saying?*
—Alain de Botton

TECHNICALLY, WE DID HAVE a roof on the house in Port Townsend, but a tarp would have provided more protection. The shingles had been overtaken by moss, and what few remained had a disconcerting tendency to let go in stormy weather and fly about the neighborhood like disoriented crows, their curling black edges flapping in the wind.

We could not move forward in the renovation without a solid roof—there would be no point in putting in systems or finishes that would then be ruined by leaks. But the foundation had taken so long that we had sunk to the bottom of the roofers' priority list, and now the autumn rains had started early, which made the roofers' schedule, always weather-dependent, even more unpredictable.

But finally, the roofers called—we had a date. Excited by the prospect of forward movement after so much waiting, George wrote a schedule on the interior of a wall, an exhilarating succession of dominoes—electrical, insulation, drywall, tile, cabinets, carpet—each one ticking us toward the finish line. An ambitious thing, it had us painted by Thanksgiving, trimmed by Christmas.

We forgot a major superstition of house renovation: Never write a schedule on a wall. Especially not with a Sharpie.

The roofing company canceled, set a new date, then canceled, again and again. Once more, we were playing the waiting game.

IF A HEARTH IS the heart of a house and the job of the foundation is to hold it up, then the role of a roof is to keep us safe. The book *Patterns of Home* declares, "More than any other single element, the form of the roof . . . carries the look and meaning of shelter, of home." In American Sign Language, the word *home* is based on the sign for *roof*, a gable made by the fingertips of two hands, protecting the space in between.

The reason roofs are peaked, sloped, and angled is to hold back the weather. Snow and rain slide down and fall off, leaving the inside of the house untouched. In their own way, roofs protect us from the weight of the world, while their shape sends the message that we can survive whatever comes down upon us. The Chinese ideogram series that ends up with *family* begins with the gable of a roof.

The idea is so iconic that when Le Corbusier built his houses for workers, a streamlined series of flat-roofed boxes, the workers then quickly turned around and added the elements that meant "home" to them—shutters, porches, and, of course, peaked roofs. Critics were appalled, but there is no dissuading us from our basic emotional needs. Without that feeling of protection, it's hard to sleep, to live, to build the family that grows beneath the roof.

IT WAS ALMOST THE middle of September. I woke up in our house in Seattle to the sound of our daughter running down the hall.

"Someone's flown a plane into a building in New York," she yelled out.

Groggy with sleep, I suggested that perhaps one of her friends was playing a joke on her. But Kate was insistent, and we turned on the television just in time to watch the first tower of the World Trade Center fall. In that moment, our narrative as Americans was changed.

WE CREATE STORIES WITH beginnings, middles, and ends, and then cast them out into the world, talismans against the reality that life does not always tie up neatly, that it can come at you sideways, take away your breath, your life, your sustaining belief that everything will end up okay. We write our stories on paper, like wishes on New Year's, and send them into the world.

Minoru Yamasaki, the architect who designed the twin towers, was, ironically enough, the same man who had created Pruitt-Igoe in Saint Louis, the low-income housing complex that was demolished so soon after its creation. In Yamasaki's narrative, the towers would be a symbol of peace that would give humankind a sense of pride and nobility. He designed the towers, what would be the tallest buildings in the world at that time, to be ageless and immune to the forces of nature. What he never counted on was man. One of the terrorists who orchestrated the 9/11 attacks was an Egyptian who had studied architecture himself and saw a different story in the twin towers—the antithesis of communal marketplaces, a way of life he believed was threatened by corporate culture in the United States. Two narratives for the two towers.

I WAS SUPPOSED TO go out to Port Townsend the day the towers fell, but it didn't happen. I didn't want to leave my family. I spent the day watching the news, as the second tower came down, then the third plane, and the fourth. Everything was falling from the sky, taking lives and our collective sense of security with it.

I went the following day, but it was a strange and disconcerting journey. The ferry had a military escort cruising alongside it. Once I reached land again, I found that the roads were lined with US flags: big ones fluttering on poles, and stiff little plastic ones attached to mailboxes. I drove between them, red, white, and blue, stark against the grey weather, as I listened to the news.

I took the same route through town that I always did—ending in the road that led straight up the hill, with the house greeting you from a distance. The alternate route was a circuitous one, with the house coming as a surprise at the end of a particularly large curve. It was an equally pretty option, but I always took the first one; I wanted to know, blocks before I arrived, that the house was still standing. I needed time to prepare myself if it wasn't. Over the months we'd owned the house, taking the first route had turned into a kind of superstition—as long as I went that way, the house would be there, I told myself.

IF YOU THINK ABOUT all that can happen during building construction, it seems almost logical that there are so many rituals and superstitions connected to it. If you are lifting a thirty-five-ton house above your head, it only makes sense not to shave if you have even the slightest belief that not shaving will bring you luck. And if following a certain route keeps your heart from pounding for an entire two-hour drive, well then I say, do it.

Most building rituals happen at a pivotal moment in the process, as a way of fending off harm or celebrating completion. The idea of placing objects under the first stone set in a foundation can be found in cultures all around the world. Often the object is a coin, but herbs, charms, the relics of saints, and sometimes even time capsules can find their way into the structure. I remember when our house was being lowered back down, I saw Roman slip a dollar bill onto the top of the concrete foundation just before the house settled into place. I asked him what he was doing, and he just smiled.

The history of building rituals was not always so benign, however. Superstitions run deep during times when life seems perilous. The coin or herb at a cornerstone harks back to the days of ritual sacrifice given to appease the spirit of a place. There are ancient legends in Japan of "human pillars"—maidens buried alive in or near a building to protect it from attack. Animals have been sacrificed as well: some traditions call for a cat to be buried underneath the floorboards, or the blood of a chicken poured across a threshold. In a truly creative attempt to avoid violence, builders would try to capture the shape of a shadow, or the "measure of a man," and put it underneath the foundation stone, instead of an actual body. The guilt here is only deferred, however, as it was believed that any man whose shadow was caught in this way would die within a year.

These days, we're more inclined to record and promote, and a cornerstone of major buildings is often something quite visible, with the name and date carved in it for all to see. But the building traditions still continue, changing and shifting as rituals often do.

THE *ENCYCLOPAEDIA OF SUPERSTITIONS, Folklore, and the Occult Sciences of the World*, first published in 1903, relates a Bulgarian belief concerning a house spirit—an entity created during the construction process, which watches over the house "as long as it stands." If any house could make me believe it had a spirit, it was ours in Port Townsend. Ever since we became the owners, things had happened that couldn't quite be explained. There was the delicate antique woman's watch that inexplicably fell out of the living room ceiling the day after I'd lost my sturdy workman's version to the ivy. The forty-year-old Father's Day card that appeared in the kitchen, months after we'd cleaned out all the trash. The tree pruner who arrived unannounced at the front door just as I was contemplating the unkempt branches of our now-ivyless orchard.

For that matter, there was no reason we should have found the house at all. We'd just set out, driven two blocks up a hill, and there it was. As simple as that. Over and over, it's felt as if the house was watching out for us.

ON THAT SEPTEMBER 12, I spent a lot of time standing outside, staring at the house. The world still felt unreal, but more than ever I felt the need to take care of this structure. I couldn't put the planes back in the sky, but I could try to save this one thing, to make it whole and beautiful once again.

For months, we'd been debating what should replace the asbestos shingles that were by now almost completely gone. We wanted to re-create the original house as much as possible, but in its current condition there was no way of knowing what the exterior siding had once been, and we hadn't been able to find any photos. I'd even gone down to the local history museum and plowed my way through album after album of pictures. Nothing.

"We need to make a decision soon," George told me as we were leaving at the end of the day. "You'll just have to go with your gut, I guess." My gut told me wood shingles, but Ben suggested that was mostly because I loved old beach houses.

I got in the car and started the drive home, no more decisive than when I'd arrived—but halfway out of town, I realized I'd left my notebook behind, so I turned around. As I pulled back up to the house, I saw a white-haired man standing in our front yard, looking up at the roof.

"Can I help you?" I asked. It was not unusual for people to stop and stare; we were still quite the sight.

"My father used to live here when he was a boy," the man said. "I've got photos. Would you like to see them?"

He showed them to me, a series of sepia-toned moments. In them, the house rises up, its walls straight and strong—and covered in wood shingles.

MR. KING ENDED UP being a delightful man, and his photos provided a different, gentler chapter in the house's story. Talking to him helped mitigate the slight feeling of creepiness that had lingered even after all the trash was cleared out. It wasn't the house itself that felt that way. Sometimes possessions can leave ghosts behind even after they're gone, and I, for one, wanted to be rid of them.

In fact, when we'd decided to move the upstairs bathroom into the northeast corner, there had been more to it for me than practicality.

The bedroom there had contained some of the most disturbing objects in the house, and even with the trash gone, the feeling in the room persisted. It felt like it still needed cleansing, and I liked the idea of water running through that space, washing everything away.

A couple weeks after I'd met Mr. King, I got a call from George. I'd stayed home in Seattle that day; since 9/11, I'd found myself doing that more often, wanting to be near the kids. I told myself that things had slowed on the site again anyway as we continued to wait for the roofers. I was hoping George was calling to tell me that they were finally coming, but his voice sounded odd, not celebratory at all.

"Something happened," he said.

My heart dropped. My mind went into overdrive, all the horrible scenarios I'd ever imagined, playing in fast-forward through my mind.

"We were pressure-testing the plumbing," George continued, "and the cap on the upstairs toilet just blew. I've never had that happen before, I swear. Anyway, all this water came pouring out, and it went down the front stairway and out the door."

"That's weird," I said. "I was just thinking about how the house needed a good washing out."

"Well, stop thinking," George said sternly. "Because it's happened twice now."

THREE WEEKS, FOUR, FIVE. No roofers. Winter was on the horizon, the skies grey and wet, day after day. The schedule George had written on the wall was now a daily rebuke, dates slipping one after another. At times, it seemed we'd be lucky to have a roof by Thanksgiving.

Back at home in Seattle, things were quieting, becoming peaceful. We'd all had a major reset in perspective that fall. In addition, the breaks that Kate and I had had from each other had given us room to breathe, and without his mother always there, ready to do everything for him, Ry was growing into himself. I was growing into myself, too. In a bout of homesickness for Italy, I had taken a cooking class one night. As I'd stood with the rest of the students, our hands deep in ingredients we would soon feed one another, I looked around that kitchen and wondered: What would happen to a group of strangers if they continued doing that intimate activity of cooking together?

And just like that, an idea for a book fell into my head, and in the weeks that followed, after decades of trying and failing to write, I suddenly had characters showing up in my mind, one after another. I didn't write them down yet—I still had a house to renovate—but at night when I couldn't sleep, instead of imagining catastrophes, I thought of those characters, and the dark, still hours turned into something beautiful.

Perhaps that is what rituals and stories really are—another place to put our anxious minds. A safe space inside yourself in a world that doesn't always make sense, that can terrify you or break your heart. Faced with such a world, I created a cooking school in my imagination. Our architect believed in an alternate universe where humans were monitored by a more intelligent species. In Japan, at the end of framing, workers sometimes shoot an arrow northwest, to send away the evil spirits. Our thoughts, our worries, go with those arrows, with those stories, carried away by myths of our own making.

THE CREW HAD DONE all they could; framing, plumbing, and windows were all in. Choices had been made for everything from appliances to faucets. All we needed was two or three days of good weather, and roofers—one little push and we could fly toward the finish.

"We gotta catch a break sometime," George said. But it didn't happen.

One afternoon, I found myself in the house alone. The days were rapidly getting shorter, and the sky was almost dark at five o'clock. I stood there in my water-washed house. Although the house had felt better since the plumbing tsunami, there was still something that wasn't quite right. Perhaps it sounds strange, but it felt as if the house was waiting for something, and that nothing would go forward until that happened.

I walked through the house, hearing the sound of my footsteps against the wooden floor. When I got to the front door, I listened for a moment. Everything was quiet.

"What do you want?" I asked the house. "Why won't you let the roofers come?"

I looked around at the framed-in walls that were waiting for the insulation and drywall that couldn't happen without a roof—and then suddenly I remembered. When we were taking down the plaster and lath, I'd promised the house that I would put a note inside the walls for whoever would come after us. And I hadn't.

AS LONG AS THERE have been walls, people have put objects inside them—love letters, shoes, board games. Bottles filled with hair and nail clippings and red thread, created to keep a witch at bay. A hidden doorframe for a future room. George told me about one house he'd worked on that had been insulated entirely with first-edition books— not so valuable at the time of construction, but worth more than the house itself when they were discovered one hundred years later. One lucky soul found a figurine of a former Russian czar, which was later auctioned for $5 million.

We put things in walls because we are scared, because we have secrets, because we have the basic human need to communicate with people we may never meet. People who will open a wall in the future and understand that we were once here.

I knew what I needed to do then, but I didn't want to just jot a quick note. I wanted my contribution to our walls to mean something to whoever found it later, but also to mean something to us now. So I went home and gathered photos of our family that showed us in every place we had lived and been happy, and I brought them back to Port Townsend.

I stood in the living room, near the framed-in wall by the front door. I took the note I had written, welcoming whoever found it, and put it in an envelope. Then I carefully added the photos, one after another. I looked at the story they told, the family in them, the four of us with our arms around each other. The kids growing up—in Seattle, in Italy, but always with us. And that was when I understood.

In the year and a half that it had taken to negotiate with the heirs, to get the house cleaned out, the foundation in, the renovation even to this point, more had changed than the house. When we'd first discovered it, we had been in the turmoil of relocation, casting about for roots. But in the time since, roots had grown. For Ben and the kids, that had meant in Seattle. They'd rediscovered friends and found routines that brought them joy and a sense of belonging. Their lives had a structure, located in a place that was not here.

It was about to get even trickier. We had recently gotten word that a new Seattle public high school would be opening, a school that was small, urban, experimental. The opportunity it presented was like nothing we could find in Port Townsend at that time, and exactly the kind of thing that Kate would love. Through the luck of a lottery, she had the opportunity to go the next year, and I saw her excitement at the prospect. Conceivably, we could have had her live with friends while we moved out to Port Townsend—I had done that myself for a period of time during one of my family's relocations. But I didn't want that. The distance away from my daughter had taught me how much I wanted to be with her.

And our son, who hated transitions more than just about anything, was finally happy again. Fully landed in his own country. I thought of all the times my parents had moved me as a child. The wrench of it, and the years it had taken me to find myself again each time. Living in Italy had been worth that cost, but suddenly I didn't know how to justify this one.

We had gotten this house to make roots. In the process of working on it, I had found them. My roots were my kids, my husband—and they were in Seattle.

I looked up and around me. This was not the story I had imagined. Ben and I had fallen in love with this house back when it was ugly and beaten and sad. In that storybook of my childhood, we would save the house and bring it a family to love.

But real life is not stories. Sometimes in real life, the endings are not what you expect. Sometimes, home is not a place.

"Really?" I said. "That's what I'm supposed to do?"

The house waited, patient.

I took the envelope and nailed it to the interior of the wall.

"I'll come back," I said. "I promise."

The roofers arrived the next day.

Part IV:

DOMUS

THE EMPTY NEST

Each one of us has, somewhere in his heart,
the dream to make a living world, a universe.
—Christopher Alexander

THERE IS A POINT in the crossing between Edmonds and Kingston where the two ferries pass going in opposite directions. Bright white and green, they stand out in crisp contrast to the silvers and blues of the water and sky, the dark slopes of islands that surround you like the backs of great, solemn whales. The ferries glide by one another, mirror images, and it is like occupying two spaces at the same time. It always makes me wonder: What if there is another me on that other boat, having an opposite life?

Scientists theorize about parallel universes, alternate realities. There is not yet any definitive proof, but what I know is that when I am looking at a mirror ferry, it feels like a recognition of an alternate possibility that makes me ponder all of them. Who would I have been if we hadn't found that house in Port Townsend? Who would I have been if we'd decided to stay there?

IN QUANTUM MECHANICS, PARALLEL universes are divided by a single event. I always think that to be a quantum event in a person's life, the occurrence must come out of the blue, unplanned except at the most subliminal level—the blast of a cue ball hitting an impossible-angle shot, sending your life hurtling off in a new direction.

My first real quantum event happened at the end of my senior year in college, when I ran into Ben on a set of stairs. It was not a meet-cute love-at-first-sight thing—life is generally more complicated than that. Ben and I had known each other for almost a year at that point. He ran the telephone switchboard for the dormitory in which I was the head resident, which meant he spent a good portion of his time right outside my apartment door. He was, in many ways, my best friend, there as I'd worked my way through one strange romance after another that year and made my plans for the future. He was firmly ensconced in a relationship of his own, with a woman who could have been his twin. He was younger than me, my height, an artist who was full of adventure and grand schemes—while I tended to go for diplomats in training and tall guys who made me feel safe. Absolutely not guys who had girlfriends. Still, it seemed as if Ben and I talked about anything and everything during those long evenings around the switchboard.

On the night of the quantum event, I'd been crying. I was leaving a party, at the end of a Dickensian *Christmas Carol* kind of night that had included encounters with just about every bad boyfriend I'd ever had. I just wanted to go back to my room and sleep, and then I wanted to graduate and get the heck out of Dodge.

But there was Ben at the base of the steps. He walked me back to the dorm. We talked for the entire weekend, and at the end of it we kissed. The ancient Romans said that *domus* meant both person and place, but I believe a person can *be* a place, too. In that moment, Ben became my home, and he has been ever since.

Two decades, two children, and two relocations later, we found the house in Port Townsend—another unexpected event. Leaving it behind had been a choice between lives, between homes.

But now I was on the ferry, going back.

IT HAD BEEN SIX years since we'd finished the renovation. Once the roof went on, the rest had flowed remarkably smoothly—drywall, paint, trim, shingles—each one a step both toward and away from the house. By the spring of 2002 we were done. We found renters, good ones, and I gave them the keys I thought I would hold. I had thought it would break my heart, but as I drove off that last day, what I felt was an extraordinary gratitude. Even if I wasn't able to live in it, that house had brought me home. And I knew, too, that I would do whatever it took to keep it, so I could come back someday.

I returned to the city and my family. We made a life, a good one. Ben got a new job, and the kids clattered their way through high school, growing tall and independent. Fledging, our friends called it, and indeed our children were like birds, flapping away from us, all wings and bright eyes.

I was growing, too. One day, not long after I returned to Seattle, I'd been driving car pool when I heard a story on the radio about life coaches—that was a new thing at the time. The man who was being interviewed was talking about an alternative approach to viewing careers.

"You need to think about the things that bring you satisfaction in your life," he said. "It doesn't matter which one earns your money. The trick is to meet as many of those needs as possible."

It was perhaps not a quantum event, but it altered my life anyway. At the time, I was writing copy for hire, work that paid almost nothing. My own writing had never sold. I did the contract work mostly so I could claim an identity as a writer—but I could feel all those bland sentences slowly leaching the creativity from my words.

When I got home, I made a list of what I loved: my family, writing, cooking, houses. I thought about going to culinary school, but restaurant hours are awful for someone with children. Houses, though—that was an interesting thought. I'd learned a lot during our renovation that I could use to help buyers and sellers. Being a real estate agent could be far more lucrative than writing, and with two houses to support and the kids aiming for college, we needed the money. If I flipped the equation—tried making my living from houses instead—I could take cooking lessons on the side and write without the pressure of publication.

Once again, it was almost astonishing how easily things fell into place. I found I loved real estate—it was as energizing and demanding as the renovation had been, which made my reentry into Seattle life easier. And over the next six years, when I got breaks between clients, I worked on my cooking-school stories. I never expected anyone other than maybe my mother to read them, but writing them made me happy. And during that time, as my children headed out of childhood and I lost my father and dear friends to illness, I learned to listen to life a little better.

Unlike quantum events, irony can, or at least should, be foreseen. After all, irony is irony because all the elements are already there waiting for you. So perhaps I should have foreseen that in the ultimate act of irony, it was the book about the cooking school, the one I wrote only for myself, that finally sold. The contract was for two novels, including one I had yet to write. I didn't know what the other book would be—all I knew was that I had a year to complete it.

AND THAT IS WHERE the house in Port Townsend came in again. Out of the blue, our renters emailed to say they were leaving in September.

A fantasy bloomed in my mind—I imagined going to Port Townsend a couple days a week, like I used to, but this time I would be writing rather than slinging a sledgehammer. I could hunker down, get words done. It was a long commute for an office, and it would be tight financially, but the idea fizzed in my bloodstream. All that quiet. The space. The house.

"Can I have the house?" I said to Ben. "Just for a year?"

And we leapt, again.

NOW, I WAS ON the ferry, heading toward the house in Port Townsend. I'd waited years for this. There had been times when we'd come close to selling—it would have been the practical thing to do, after all—but we never had. Every time, something had happened that made it possible to hold on to it. A windfall at work, a new and perfect renter just when we needed one. But there was more to it than luck. I'm not the kind of person to have an affair, but at times I longed for that house in a way that felt almost unseemly. I would shove the emotions down, but the house was always in the back of my mind, waiting.

So it should have felt like triumph to be returning to the house, but suddenly it was the furthest thing from it. In the month since our renters had given notice, we had dropped Ry off for his freshman year in college—the first time both he and Kate had been gone. The house in Seattle shook with their absence, and me along with it. I didn't know what to do without their routines shaping mine, without the warmth of their bodies, the sound of their voices in the house. I was a forty-nine-year-old premenopausal woman, suddenly without children. What I did have was a deadline I didn't know how to meet and a book I didn't know if I could write.

Then, two days before I was due to head to the house in Port Townsend, the stock market crashed, spectacularly. This time, we hadn't cashed out our savings for a trash-filled house. And I'd just quit real estate, the only secure income I'd ever had, to write full-time. We had two kids in college, and we needed both of their parents to be working, hard.

Now, Ben was in the ferry line behind me, driving our camper bus, filled with a folding table, a big chair, a futon mattress, and a few pots and pans—supplies for my writing life. I looked out across the water and saw the mirror ferry coming toward me, and I wondered what the hell I was doing.

IT'S AN ODD THING about the house in Port Townsend. The first time we were ever inside, the smells were horrifying, and until we'd cleaned out the trash and gotten rid of the plaster and lath, I'd spent much of my time in a respirator. But the day we finished the reno-vation, as I was closing the front door for what I knew would be a long time, I noticed a remarkable scent—a combination of baking bread and sunshine, the most pure and loving fragrance I'd ever encountered.

"Do you smell that?" I asked George, but he just looked at me, puzzled.

I figured it would go away as soon as the renters moved in and cooked their own food, but now as I opened the door to the empty house, there was that scent again.

Ben and I carried in the few pieces of furniture—a strange reversal of our trash clean-out years before. And then Ben left, dashing to catch a ferry and go back to work, and I was standing in the house, alone.

EXPERTS ARE QUICK TO tell you that empty-nest syndrome is not a clinical diagnosis. It is, instead, a "phenomenon"—one they say has upsides as well as down. When I look for synonyms for *phenomenon*, I find *stunner* and *miracle*. I also find *paradox*, which seems appropriate.

Faced with a hollow house, parents are encouraged to fill it with plans of their own. As I stood in our living room in Port Townsend, I thought perhaps I had taken that advice a bit too literally. The house was the emptiest of nests. The walls were white, and all the trappings of family were nonexistent—no photographs on the fridge, no couch that kids had sprawled on, no dishes in the sink, no smells of Ry's late-night macaroni-and-cheese feasts. The floors were bare, and the sound of my feet echoed without the muffling effect of their lives. All I had were plans.

I set my writing chair in front of the dining room window that looked out over the orchard, to the water. The scent of the house lingered around me. I opened my laptop.

There is another synonym for phenomenon: *one for the books.*

"Okay," I said, and started to type.

AFTER YEARS OF FITTING my writing into the nooks and crannies of my life, suddenly I had an astonishing expanse of time. It rolled out before me like the view from the window. I fell into a predictable routine—I would get up early, make a cup of coffee, take a seat by the big window, and wait for the characters to come. One by one, they claimed their stories—parallel universes made of words. Perhaps it was because the space was so exactly empty that the characters came so easily, without the hooks of to-do lists or even the internet to get caught on as they found their way to me.

On the days of the week when I was in Port Townsend, I was a writer, and only that. When I was in Seattle, I did the rest of my life. Before, I had always felt guilty that I was writing when there were errands to run or dishes to wash, and the reverse was also true. Now, cued by geography, I did one role at a time and my productivity skyrocketed.

THERE WERE, OF COURSE, times when I did get stuck, when I couldn't see or hear where a character should go next. I learned quickly enough that forcing the words only wrote me into a corner—in my desire to hit a daily word count, I was shoving my characters into plot points they could never live inside. They would grumble, go sideways, go silent.

When that happened, I learned to put the laptop down and head out for a walk, letting the sound of the waves and the motion of my feet jostle the ideas around in my head. Outside, it was easier to let go of the control, to listen and allow the characters to figure out where they wanted to be.

I began to carry a small notebook with me so I could write down ideas when they arrived. Gradually, over the months and miles, it got to the point where walking was as much a part of writing as moving my fingers across the keys.

I'M NOT THE FIRST writer to be a walker, not by a long shot. It's been said that William Wordsworth walked almost 175,000 miles in his life. Aristotle used to give his lectures on foot (and Steve Jobs did the same with his meetings). Charles Dickens maintained the same writing schedule I did—writing in the morning and walking in the afternoon, although his walks were said to be in the twenty-to-thirty-mile category. I can't imagine.

There are scientific reasons behind our desire for movement. Walking is particularly helpful for what is called "divergent thinking," the brainstorming kind, which aims for many possible solutions rather than one answer. In a 2014 Stanford University experiment, participants were asked to come up with new and novel uses for a known object. Their creative output was raised by 60 percent when they were walking as opposed to sitting. In another experiment, where participants were tasked with generating complex analogies, 100 percent of the participants who walked outside could come up with at least one, as opposed to 50 percent of those seated inside.

The theory here is that walking allows the brain to focus on something it already knows how to do, which gives the rest of your mind free rein to wander. Which is all to say that if you are stuck in the middle of writing a book or trying to figure out your life, perhaps the best thing you can do is walk.

And so I did. Mile after mile after mile. Port Townsend is tailor-made for pedestrians, woven together by paths that meander over hills and around the town. There is a sense of mystery as you enter one of these trails for the first time; you're never quite sure where you'll come out. I made a pact with myself—any time there was a path, I took it. If I got lost, all the better.

Walking became second nature, and I got used to parking my car when I arrived and not touching it again until it was time to leave. Anything I needed was within a mile or two, and the streets of Port Townsend seemed to belong to people more than cars, anyway. As I walked, I got stronger and happier—and the words flowed.

WRITERS AREN'T THE ONLY ones who are made better by living in a walkable city. Studies done using data from Walk Score, a company that determines the walkability of US cities, have shown that if you reside in a pedestrian-friendly neighborhood, your likelihood of becoming obese drops by 25 percent. General satisfaction with your life trends upward, as well; in survey after survey, walkable cities slam-dunk the ones where the inhabitants are reliant on cars. It's easy to see why. It's estimated that today, a cyclist in London will move faster than most drivers—who will also each spend 106 days of their lives searching for parking spots. In Seattle, which in 2017 was ranked second in the nation for evening rush-hour congestion, a driver with a one-hour commute will waste an extra 148 hours per year just trying to get home.

But there's another, less quantifiable benefit to walking. On those afternoons exploring Port Townsend, I gained a feeling for the terrain and the community in a way I had never experienced driving around Seattle. While a GPS system relieves a driver of having to pay attention to the route, and a car speeds us past the details of shopwindows and people's faces and the weather, walking gives us an intimacy with our environment that sinks in deep. In Port Townsend, my walks were navigated by sensory details: a fence decorated with brightly colored coffee mugs, the feel of damp earth beneath my shoes, the smell from the local bakery early in the morning. My senses woke up and reached out, connecting me physically to that small part of the world.

I SPENT THE BETTER part of twelve months in Port Townsend writing that second novel. Once again, the house had become my place to fig-ure out who I was. It provided both an empty nest and a perch, refuge and prospect as I looked toward what came next. Because in reality I was doing a lot more than writing a book. I was being on my own, in many ways for the first time in my life. I had grown up surrounded by siblings, then a husband, then children—always observed, always observing. But this was different. In that empty space, I was just myself. I made my own context. I learned to ride the waves of my changing hormones and welcome what the bright and dark moods could bring to my writing. I practiced having opinions dependent upon no one else's needs. I would stay up until two in the morning if the writing was going well, or get up at four and write into the light.

You might think that all this was a recipe for divorce—and indeed, some of our friends thought Ben and I were attempting a trial separation, given the logistics of the situation. But in fact, the opposite was true. Allowed the space to be a writer, I was a better wife. I was more likely to take the initiative, to do things that made me happy, and to state my needs, rather than wait, frustrated, for Ben to intuit what I wanted. He'd been asking for those things for years. And if my being away meant he got a few evenings on his own to indulge his cravings for junk food, well, that was just a bonus.

AT THE END OF that year, I finished the book and put up the FOR RENT sign once again. The latter almost broke my heart, but the economic depression was still in full force. We'd managed for the year, but we still needed Ben's job in the city, and we couldn't sell our Seattle house until the market recovered again. Port Townsend would have to wait, one more time.

The one thing I didn't have to wait for was a renter. Fifteen minutes after I put up the sign, just as I was collecting my things to leave, a sweet young couple came to the front door. Standing on the porch, they told me they almost never took this route on their afternoon walk, but on impulse they'd gone a different way that day and seen the sign. When I invited them in to look at the house, the woman stopped in the entry, marveling.

"What's that beautiful smell?" she asked.

Her husband gazed about, puzzled.

I smiled. "I think this is yours," I told her, and held up the key.

LEAVING HOME

The question of what you want to own
is actually the question of how you
want to live your life.

—Marie Kondo

ONE YEAR, TWO, THREE. Finally, all the pieces were coming together. Both kids were truly fledged, with jobs and apartments of their own. The economy was finding its footing as well, and our backyard neighbors in Seattle asked if they could buy our house. They were a young couple with two kids, who wanted to stay in the neighborhood but needed more space. It all felt right; it was time to move.

But first—in an instance of perfect and ironic symmetry—we had to clean out our house.

BACK WHEN WE WERE clearing out the trash in the house in Port Townsend, we had set some things aside for a garage sale, although the logic of our choices had been haphazard at best. As a result, the event had had a Salvador Dalí–esque quality—the lavender padded toilet seat lined up next to fourteen fishing rods, twenty-five bowling balls, thirty-two pairs of size thirteen wing-tip shoes, a huge box of avocado-colored dishware, and another of ancient 78s, music from another time crumbling out of the vinyl.

It hadn't seemed to matter to the people who arrived and plowed through our questionable merchandise with the excitement of Black Friday shoppers. Maybe it was the thrill of finally getting inside the mystery house, or maybe it really was what we were selling, but the mood was frenzied, to put it mildly. In the midst of it all, rat number thirteen crawled out of the dining room wall. Weaving in a poisoned stupor between the feet of the crowd, it had managed to make it to the exact center of the room, where it seized up, shivered, and died, slowly, the *La Bohème* of rodent opera.

There was not even a pause in the bargaining.

After that, I'd returned to Seattle and started going through our own things with a vengeance. I even organized an annual neighborhood garage sale. Ours lacked the flair of the one in Port Townsend, but at the end of the day, the stuff was gone, which was all I'd cared about. What surprised me was how I could fill the entire front lawn, year after year. Every January, I would start at the top of our house and work my way down, a room a month, the cast-asides collecting in a corner of the basement until the sale in September. Plastic baseball bats for children long grown up. Flannel shirts from a phase of mine in college. Wedding gifts we'd never used. Six giant bottles of window cleaner. All those Legos. I'd thought I was organized, completely different from the hoarder whose life I'd so intimately touched. But every year, the front yard filled, and every year I would dig a bit deeper into the closets and the drawers. But it seemed that no matter how deep I went, there was always another layer or two or ten.

MARIE KONDO, WHOSE BOOK *The Life-Changing Magic of Tidying Up* has become an international phenomenon, would say my problem was that I was doing my winnowing all wrong. Kondo does not follow the traditional wisdom that sorting can be done an object a day, or a room a month. She believes in an all-out one-time purge—the kind that makes such a visual impact that you are forever changed, unwilling to backslide into clutter.

A hoarder would be horrified by this approach—family members who have attempted to do such a clean-out as a surprise have often seen the project backfire spectacularly. But there are plenty of us who fall into the middle ground of simply having accumulated too much. According to the *Los Angeles Times,* the typical home in the United States contains over three hundred thousand objects, while the US Department of Energy has determined that of those homeowners who have two-car garages, 32 percent of them park one car outside, and 25 percent park both, because the space inside is already filled with stuff. For these people, the results of a Kondo-like purge can indeed be life-changing.

Kondo's approach is a straightforward one: Go through each thing you own and ask yourself if it brings you joy. If it does, keep it. If it doesn't, thank it for its service and send it on its way.

She makes it sound so simple.

MY SORTING FORAYS OF the previous decade had been limited to the main floors, carefully overlooking what lay at the bottom of the stairs. Basements are where life settles, like silt drifting down from the stream above. But now we were actually selling the house, and I had no choice but to go below.

Our basement was, in general, Ben's haven—a giant storage locker of camping equipment, woodworking tools, bikes, kayaks, and a Ping-Pong table that was always covered in boxes. In the midst of it all were three black filing cabinets. Paperwork seemed an easy place to start. I opened the top drawer of the closest cabinet and encountered my income tax return from 1982.

Well, then.

I went out and bought a shredder. I brought it home, a metal canister the size of the blue air compressor for the power chisel Ry and I had used years before, when we took down the chimney. I held the pages of the tax return over the slit in the top of the shredder, and then listened to its sharp teeth grind their way through my past.

One file after another, until I hit the recommended seven-year limit. All those years when I was a barely paid teaching assistant, slogging my way through graduate school. The more than a decade when I was a stay-at-home mom and the manuscripts weren't selling. There were so many documents that the shredder would start emitting ominous electrical smells, and I would have to give my little factory of destruction a break, thank it for its service.

In the middle of the files, I found the letter I had received from the Social Security Administration on my forty-fifth birthday, delineating my past earnings and predicting my total future income at $0. Into the shredder it went, munched into thin white strips, which I stuffed into black plastic bags along with the rest until the basement resembled a hayfield during threshing season. A harvest of the unnecessary.

In the bottom drawer, I found my dissertation, typed in Courier, the paper yellowed. One hundred twenty pages of esoteric literary analysis, an approach that had fit me no better than the pointy black stilettos I'd bought for a party I didn't even want to attend. I'd gone to graduate school because it had seemed a legitimate way to stay near writing, when all I'd really wanted to do was create new words on blank pages. I'd spent seven years turning myself into someone I wasn't. I'd known it the moment I graduated—probably long before—and yet I had still kept the dissertation through all those decades since, moving it from my desk to a closet, and then steadily down the levels until it landed in the basement filing cabinet. Now I had to decide, once and for all, what to do with the thing.

WHILE I WAS SORTING through our possessions, I'd been reading Xorin Balbes's *SoulSpace*, hoping for inspiration. Published in the United States several years before Kondo's book, *SoulSpace* covers much of the same territory, although the two authors come at it from slightly different perspectives—Balbes leaning toward a California interior-designer spirituality, while Kondo demonstrates an impressive tendency toward OCD behavior. The basic premise of both authors' books, however, is a simple one—keep only those things that bring you true joy, so that when you walk through your house, you are brought alive by the objects you see and touch. It means asking, *Do I love this thing with my soul?* A truly affirmative answer comes from a deep and certain feeling of recognition that has nothing to do with the sparkling fizz of acquisition or the finding of a good deal. One is nourishment; the other, sugar.

It also means acknowledging the way some objects can hold you back. Balbes's book includes fascinating descriptions of clients' homes, and his approach can feel like a psychological analysis done through a homeowner's possessions. In the case of Lili, a successful businesswoman who couldn't seem to find love, Balbes found the answer in her house. As he walked through its rooms, he noticed that the bed was large enough for two, but one side was pushed against the wall. In the living room, there was an uncomfortable couch and a single good reading chair. You get the idea—but what is surprising, or perhaps not, is that Lili never saw it herself. When she moved the bed, pitched the old couch, and bought a second comfortable chair, she opened up her life to a new partner.

Was it the more welcoming furniture, or her acknowledgment of her behavior that brought about the change? I think it was both, in that way that our emotions and possessions naturally interact, reinforcing and reminding us of our best and worst tendencies. Balbes and Kondo would suggest we aim for the former and discard the latter.

STANDING THERE IN THE basement, I flipped through the pages of my dissertation, smelling the mustiness inside. I could keep it as a symbol of accomplishment, leaving the pages in the drawer, muttering away like Rochester's wife. Or I could look about me, at the life I had made since, the one I would choose over and over again.

The dissertation soared across the room into the recycling bin.

And with that, the floodgates were opened. Those black stilettos—gone. The garden gnome that creeped me out but was a gift from a relative who might visit someday found a new home at Goodwill. Then there was the leather-bound volume of Shakespeare plays, given to me by a boyfriend I had long wanted to forget—but what respectable English major gets rid of Shakespeare? Me, apparently.

It felt astonishingly good.

WEEKS LATER, AFTER AN embarrassingly large number of trips to the dump and a gigantic final garage sale, the possessions we had chosen to take with us were finally packed in boxes and ready to go. Ben and I rented a U-Haul truck and put out the word to family and friends: *Come help us move. We have pizza and beer.*

In all our relocations—from Los Angeles to Seattle, from one apartment or house to the next—we had never hired movers. You could say that we were penny-pinchers, and you'd probably be right. But there was something more to it. Moving your own things—lifting and carrying their weight—is an opportunity to know in your muscles how much you have. And having others help you, and helping them in turn, is a way to build community, something we Americans used to do a lot more of.

I read once about an island off the southern coast of Chile called Chiloé. It is small—mostly inhabited by fishermen and farmers. When a family needs to move house, due to rising tides or a desire for more farmable land, the community takes the action literally. They come together and transport the building itself, in a tradition called a *minga*. Like an American barn raising, it is an activity done without payment, with the knowledge that you, too, will be helped sometime in the future.

I thought about the friends and family who had been with us along the way in this journey toward the house in Port Townsend— who had helped clean out the trash and sledgehammered walls and planted grass seed and painted shingles. Now, hands that we knew and loved were lifting boxes, sending them, and us, on our way.

IT HELPED IN MORE ways than one to have friends with us as we got ready to leave. It is a hard thing to move, whether or not you love where you are going. My father had a rule when making major decisions in his life: You need a reason to go, and a reason to leave. Fleeing without a destination, or leaping toward something without an understanding of why you are going, will always leave you slightly off balance. But if you work your way through both reasons, you will have to look both forward and back, a classic push-me/pull-you thought process that helps you face the future, ready and secure.

I knew where I was going. I knew why I was leaving. But what my father's saying didn't tell me was what to do with all the emotional reasons to stay anyway. Because the thing about houses is that regardless of their layout, regardless of whether you have fought them or flowed into them—they hold your family. The house in Seattle had held ours for twenty-two years. Our son was a baby, our daughter a toddler, when I had seen the FOR SALE BY OWNER ad in the paper and known that this old, rangy house, only four blocks away from our too-small one, could give us the space we needed. When we moved in, the rooms echoed around us, and we filled them with our lives.

Houses are made of wood and glass, but they are also made of the events that happen within them. The dining room was dark, but it was also the setting for candlelit family dinners and evenings when Ry's friends would spread out their board games and play late into the night, their laughter bouncing up the stairs. The kitchen had been our Grand Central Station, full of high chairs and dog bowls, and during its own renovation—while the walls were still studs and the floors plywood—it was where we hosted my favorite birthday party for Ben, using sawhorses to make a table, covering it with a white linen tablecloth, and surrounding it with friends. And then there was the piano room, with its fake Art Deco wallpaper, which we swore we'd replace right away and never did, the room that never did hold a piano but where I'd watched every episode of *Sex and the City* with my daughter during the summer before she went to college—because she'd wanted to, and because I'd wanted to sit there next to her on the couch for as long as we could.

Years before, I'd collected photos of our lives and put them in an envelope in the wall by the front door of the house in Port Townsend. What I didn't know was how to take the memories that lived in the walls of this one.

BY LATE AFTERNOON, THE U-HAUL truck and Ben and our kids and friends were gone. I was on task to do the last cleanup, but before that, I went next door to see my neighbor. Rachel and I had raised our children together, providing a sanity check for each other on long and rainy afternoons filled with pent-up toddlers and then teenagers. For years, when our husbands' careers were new and time intensive, she and I traded off cooking dinner for each other, plates delivered through a gate we had built in the fence between our two backyards. Once a week—a grown-up meal with salad, in a life otherwise ruled by macaroni and cheese. It's funny how much those things matter.

Our kids were gone now, our houses quiet. In her kitchen, Rachel handed me a gin and tonic. We went into her backyard and sat under the oak tree that had grown over the decades into the behemoth of the neighborhood. She couldn't bear to cut it down, so she had given up her sunny vegetable beds and planted a shade garden under its boughs, and we sat among the ferns and talked. And then, because children are never fully fledged, she went to pick up her son at the airport, and I went back to the Seattle house one more time.

IT'S AMAZING HOW FULL an empty house can feel. It was as if I could see our family more clearly now, as if without furniture there was space for the memories to breathe. I cleaned each room, wiping down the surfaces, washing the floors. When I was finished, I went through the rooms again, taking a photograph of each one. The late August light was coming in sideways, the way I love it, illuminating parts of the house that only saw the sun for those few hours of the year, as if every bit of the house were saying goodbye. I checked each closet and drawer for items left behind and then headed for the front door, past the sideboard with its pile of twenty duplicate keys we had collected from our children, neighbors, friends, and extended family who had been given free access to our lives. I could have left mine behind, too; the door locked on its own. But I told myself I might have to come back—perhaps I would remember that I'd left on the heat, which hadn't been turned on all summer, or that I'd forgotten the toaster I knew I'd packed a week before. So I kept the key and closed the door, hearing its funny little double click as it settled in place.

Then I walked down the stairs, got in the car, and headed north to the ferry.

THE WRITING SHED

If I were asked to name the chief
benefit of the house ... I should say:
the house shelters daydreaming.

—Gaston Bachelard

WHEN WE FIRST DISCOVERED the house in Port Townsend, my mind was still half in the plane returning from Italy, unsure, needing roots for my family but also, as much as anything, for myself. When I came back to the house the second time, I was an empty nester, unsure of myself once again. Each time, the house presented a possibility for renovation, always different, but always when I needed it most. Now as I walked up its front steps, I could feel the possibilities once more.

Thank you, I said. But whether I was thanking the house or all the intricacies of life and luck that had led us to it, allowed us to keep it again and again, I couldn't say. Perhaps they were one and the same in the end.

I opened the door, and there was that scent waiting for me.

IN THIS ITERATION OF our lives, the house would be a dwelling for two, a number we wanted to be able to expand to many without effort before contracting back—a state something like breathing. After all the sorting we'd just done, I was determined to keep things simple and purposeful, and we took our time finding the right places for our things.

We'd brought with us the small closet door on which we'd measured our children as they grew, and now we hung it on the wall just inside our back door, so the kids would greet us every time we walked in. Photos of our children and siblings and parents went on the sideboard in the dining room, so we would always eat with family. We positioned our bed so that we would wake looking out at the water, and in the nook halfway up the stairs, I put research books for future novels, a reminder each time I passed by that new worlds waited. Object by object, we settled in.

LIFE ROLLED THROUGH THE years in waves—one, three, five. Our daughter got married. Our son grew strong and tall. Ben and I lost our mothers, our dog, old friends. After every loss, every celebration, we would come back to the house and it would open its arms and fold us back in. It became the place where we lived.

I DON'T KNOW EXACTLY when it happened, when the blank-slate space I had once used solely for writing turned into a home, full of love, but also with a washer and dryer and refrigerator that needed tending, and an internet that clamored for my time like a small child. The memories of my year in the empty nest kept the bubble of creativity around me for a while, but eventually, the details of reality snuck in, as they will. I could hear them whispering between the keystrokes as I typed: *Pay attention to us. We need you more.* It became hard to discern the characters' voices that had been so clear before. My writing slowed. Circled. I worried about Alzheimer's and took herbs for memory and mental acuity, but they didn't seem to make a difference.

More and more often, I found myself looking out the window, down to the lower orchard. The ivy had been held at bay more or less, and the fruit trees stretched toward one another across a fairy circle of green grass. At the end nearest the street, however, there was now a gap where two huge trees had once stood—a sequoia and a spruce, originally planted so close together that they'd become half trees, well on their way to killing each other by the time we'd had to take them down, a few years before. But cutting a tree is a painful business, and the space where they once stood felt raw and unloved, while the seclusion of the lower yard had been obliterated. It needed something—a way to remember those evergreens and bring the magic back again.

"What if we built a writing shed?" I asked Ben.

I AM NOT THE FIRST WRITER to feel the desire for a separate space, away from the demands of the everyday. It was Virginia Woolf who gave it the moniker we use most often—*a room of one's own*—although behind her use of *one* resided a much more feminist message. I had some money that was all my own—an inheritance from my mother. I thought she would have liked the idea of a place set aside for creativity.

I wanted a small space; I think it goes back to that almost primal urge to create a fort, a hideaway, under a table or in a tree. I was not alone in that feeling, either: George Bernard Shaw's writing shed was a mere eight-by-eight feet, set on an ingenious steel turntable that could rotate with the sun. Dylan Thomas had his "word-splashed hut" perched on stilts above an estuary, with ten windows that looked out to views that swept his thoughts clean. Roald Dahl fashioned his writing retreat on Thomas's design, using the same six-by-seven footprint and angled roof—although Dahl opted for far less natural light. He wrote in a wingback chair that once belonged to his mother, cocooned by an astonishing number of pictures and books. Dahl said, "When I am in this place it is my little nest. My womb." One has to wonder what Virginia Woolf might have made of that last comment.

Michael Pollan documented the building of his own writing space in his book *A Place of My Own*. For Pollan, that bit of separation meant everything. "It might be a view of the same old life, but from out here it will look different," he wrote, "the outlines of the self a little more distinct." Pollan took his task seriously, spending time figuring out just the best site and orientation, drawing on advice from Vitruvius to feng shui. His attention to detail was meticulous and loving. You can hear the art of it in the rhythms of his sentences, as if process and product indeed became one.

As I read my way through descriptions of one author's hideaway after another, what became clear is that those set-apart spaces are invitations to creativity made real. Much like the act of walking, entering them relieves the workaday parts of our minds, allowing the rest to let go, dive in. On the old maps of the world, there was often a phrase, written above the uncharted parts: *terra incognita*, which means "unknown territory." Crossing the threshold of a dedicated writing space feels much the same. You leave the known world, your everyday self behind.

Hic sunt scriptors. Here there be writers.

YEARS AGO, I HAD the chance to go to a women's writing retreat called Hedgebrook. It is set on a pastoral island in Puget Sound, with a farmhouse as its central gathering spot. Scattered through the thirty acres of quiet, dense woods behind the farmhouse are six hobbit-sized cottages—small, private worlds, one for each resident. When you open the arched front door and walk in for the first time, it is like entering your own imagination, a nutshell that will grow trees.

At Hedgebrook, there is no commitment to write a certain num-ber of words, and yet the carefully planned design is there every step of the way to encourage creativity. The living room is small but offers a long desk to spread out research, a comfortable chair by a wood-stove, and a window seat. *We all write differently*, the design says. The kitchen is just big enough to heat a pot of tea. *Your job is not to cook for others.* The woodstove is small and requires tending. *You are capable.* A narrow ladder leads to a bed in an open loft. *Writing is part dreaming.*

The sense of having each of your needs seen and understood by the very architecture that surrounds you can bring out a similar atti-tude toward the words you write. It is not unusual to hear anecdotes of extraordinary productivity, and deep explorations into parts of the writing soul that had previously remained hidden.

I left Hedgebrook a different person than I'd arrived. The space itself had redefined me, and in the following years, whenever I felt my resolve wavering I remembered my cottage and the way it felt to be a maker of words in a place that was only for writing.

Now, in Port Townsend, I had the chance to design my own space, using everything I had learned about architecture and creativity. Down below me in the orchard, the place where the two trees once stood waited, ready for ideas.

AS A RENOVATOR AT HEART, however, I discovered it was unnerving to think of creating a structure from scratch. I spent months pondering the orchard, stalling. But what I finally understood is that no building, just like no person, ever truly starts from scratch. Every structure lives within its setting, a natural foundation before the ones we build. My setting was a troubling one—a wound in the earth where a sequoia and a spruce once grew, a gap in the circle of trees. My shed would be a chance to make things whole again. I came to see that it needed to be as much of the natural world as of the mind, a place that welcomed healing as well as creation. I still didn't know exactly what that would look like, though.

Then one day, I took a different route into town, and passed a large woodworkers' shop. Outside it stood a small square structure with a wide pane of glass running down the center of each wall. It was graceful and spare, a calm container for a busy mind. I pulled into the parking lot and got out for a closer look. The space inside was flooded with light. The walls were white; the floor and trim, natural wood. The ceiling was made of thin slats held together by delicate beams, a combination of complexity and simplicity. Against the back wall, I saw a desk—there wasn't room for much more. I felt my heart relax.

An old man came out of the shop. He was as thin as string, missing more than one tooth. Behind him I saw several young men working.

"You like it?" he asked. "That's my office."

I nodded. "Could you build me one?"

He quoted me a price so low I had to ask him twice, but he insisted.

"My name is John," he said, and we shook hands for a contract.

YOU MIGHT THINK THAT my previous experience with leaping into building would have taught me a thing or two. Alas, no. I had been so caught up in the kismet of the moment, of seeing the exact writing shed I wanted, of having this old man from a fairy tale pop out and offer to construct it for me, that I had thrown all my hard-earned lessons to the wind. I hadn't asked for references. I hadn't asked if those sturdy young men in the woodshop were actually his team (they weren't). And I hadn't asked a question so basic that it isn't even on the lists of what to ask prospective builders: Do you own a truck?

John didn't. He didn't even own a car. Ben and I didn't figure it out until the third day of construction, when John disappeared for four hours and returned with a short piece of wood in his hand. Curious, Ben asked him where he'd been.

"I had to cut this," he said, "so I walked over to my shop." It was two miles away.

This is how it works in Port Townsend, as often as not. Time slows, expands, becomes a summer spent watching an old man put one piece of wood after another into place. But if you slow down enough, you might learn that the very skinny man so carefully measuring each piece of wood is someone who worked with a world-class architect before running away to find a life with gentler rhythms. And if you listen more than talk while driving him to the hardware store—because, while building as a Zen practice is nice, you darn well aren't going to lose four hours again—you might hear a story about a slip on a roof, a broken back, a loss of all one holds dear. So if it takes four months to build a shed when two good weekends with a crew could have done the work—well, wasn't a slower life what you'd said you wanted when you bought that trash-filled house so many years ago?

BY THE END OF SUMMER, the shed was finished, a thing of beauty that turned the orchard into a secret garden once again. Eight by eight, just like George Bernard Shaw's hut, but my shed didn't need to rotate. The sun moved across the sky, glancing over the tops of the lilacs, then slipping through the cherry tree branches, coming in through one long window after another. What interior walls there were, I painted white; the world outside was green. I treated the wood trim with Minwax, and the smell permeated the space, a scent like sunshine and preservation.

We had decided against gutters—the structure was so small we didn't want to visually weigh it down—but it soon became clear that the runoff would hit the ground and splatter back up on the exterior walls. So I took the stones I had saved from that tall, tall chimney my son and I had taken down, and placed them around the perimeter of the shed, a river of rock that softened the impact of the falling water. The sequoia tree that once stood in that spot had been cut into live-edge boards, and now Ben fashioned them into bookshelves for me, their front edges curving in and out, in a graceful reminder that life rarely grows straight. And from the center of the ceiling, where it rose to a peak, I hung the last angel my mother ever gave me, years after I had children of my own. This angel is flying, her body thrust forward into the world, her arms flung back, each hand holding its own wing—a slim white bird feather.

OVER TIME, I HAVE developed a routine. I get up early and bring my coffee down the path, saying hello to the weather on the way. Most mornings, I write with an audience of deer, who wander into the orchard and watch me in bemusement. The other day, a raccoon walked by the glass door and looked in, curious. It reminds me of a book my mother used to read to me when I was young. In it, there was a little girl who wanted to play with all the animals in the woods. The simple line drawings show her chasing one after another, all to no avail. Finally, she sits down by a pond, despondent, but as she sits there striving after nothing, all the animals come close. It's a good lesson for writers, and for people in general.

In the summertime, I open the old recycled French doors of my writing shed and let in the warmer weather, but in the winter, the big windows bring the outside in while the sound of the rain on the metal roof echoes the clatter of the keyboard. When I am in this space, I am a writer only. I leave the internet and the chores behind. I dive in. At the end of the morning, I walk back up to the house and the husband I have loved for so long, and I welcome the rest of my life into me. My day is divided by a door, a threshold, my thoughts on each side of it unencumbered by the other, just as it was when I used to come out to Port Townsend simply to write.

In this new structure for my life, there is room for both parts of me, literally and figuratively—and I love that the word *room* is an architectural one, a space inside ourselves that we make with our minds.

THIS IS THE BEAUTY, the power, of architecture—it exists both outside and inside of us, a dance between structure and self. And it is when we begin to recognize the integrated relationship we have with our built environments that we can effect change. We can design dining rooms that invite families to eat together, bedrooms that foster relaxation and intimacy, living rooms where a natural flow to a garden encourages us to put down our screens and go outside. We can think about who we want to be, and then shape our homes in ways that will bring out those best qualities in us.

And it doesn't have to mean a major renovation or building project, either. There are many subtle changes that can make a big difference in your life. You can open up the space below a stairway, paint the inside a warm color, and create a hideaway for your child's imagination. You can make an alcove out of a single shelf, line it with objects you love, and give yourself a place to stop and remember who you've been. You can designate a corner of a room, or even just a chair, and dedicate it exclusively to creativity. The trick is the cue, and the way it guides your mind. Each thing you do will make a difference.

Chances are that somewhere down the line, caught up in our busy days, we might forget why we made those changes. But this is where the power of architecture comes in. Those encouragements will always be there, whether we are conscious of them or not, like secrets we slipped into the walls, messages from us to our future selves: *This is who you can be.*

THE DINNER

A building is not something you finish.
A building is something you start.
—Stewart Brand

ALMOST SEVENTEEN YEARS TO the day from when we walked in the front door of the house in Port Townsend and confronted the trash, we had a dinner.

Pastafest is our own family tradition, born out of a combination of necessity and invention and a desire to be together, as so many traditions are. It began when Kate was going to college in Canada, where they celebrate their Thanksgiving at a different time of year. She could only get the Friday off, and thus, several times we spent Thanksgiving evening waiting in a customs line at the border after picking her up. It could take so long that one year we ended up eating dinner at a McDonald's, the only quick option we could find on the long drive home. Under those bright lights, we raised our chicken sandwiches high over the Formica table and toasted the holiday with waxy paper cups filled with water.

I can no longer remember why we didn't just cook Thanksgiving dinner on Friday, but somehow we ended up with Pastafest, an event where we made pasta from scratch, all day long. It took as much effort as the Pilgrims' holiday, but somehow the resulting meal was more satisfying. Ever since the year we'd cooked a Thanksgiving dinner for

Italians in Bergamo—spreading the table with turkey and stuffing and mashed potatoes and gravy and green beans and creamed onions and cranberry sauce, and then watching their eyes fill with politely disguised horror at the cacophony of so many dishes coming out all at once—I'd been trying to reimagine Thanksgiving. It wasn't the dishes I had the problem with; it was the lack of attention you gave the meal when you stuffed it all down in twenty minutes. Maybe fifteen.

I wanted a new tradition, one that had the feel of a long Italian dinner. Which is, I suppose, how we landed on pasta.

THE TRADITIONS WE CHOOSE to celebrate say a lot about who we are. There are the obvious ones—the birthdays and Halloweens and Passovers—but there are also the others, more idiosyncratic and intimate. The nightly bedtime story. A fondue dinner, lit by candles, to celebrate the first snow of each year. An annual hike to the top of a dark mountain to watch the Fourth of July fireworks in the cities below. By repeating particular events in particular ways, we create the architecture of our families out of memories and values. We shape them and they shape us, just like houses.

And just like houses, they can be renovated, changed to fit who we are now. A new tradition in the spirit of the old, because what that turkey dinner in Italy taught me was that Thanksgiving wasn't about those particular dishes, or how well coordinated our timing was in getting them to the table. The spirit of Thanksgiving was gratitude, and whatever got you to that feeling was the holiday.

WE'VE BEEN DOING PASTAFEST for over a decade now. This year, we changed the date to January, extending the holiday season into a slow, dark month that needs a little celebration. Over time, the group around the table has extended as well. When I was growing up, holidays were immediate family only; Pastafest has changed that. This year, we had siblings and nephews, their partners, Kate's in-laws, Ry's childhood buddies, and their babies. We even had Kate's friend

Rebecca, who helped so many years ago demoing the plaster and lath. Now an assured young woman, home from a job in Washington, DC, she looked around the house in awe. It was her first time there since the day of the sledgehammers. She was the only one of us whose vision of that time had been preserved untouched, and through her eyes I was vaulted back. *How young we were then,* I thought.

This time, we created a cloud of flour instead of dust. Ry has grown into a man, a writer and a software coder—but the little boy who used to watch me cook from the vantage point of a backpack has also become our main pasta maker. That day saw him kneading pound after pound of dough and sending it through the roller, creating flat sheets of pasta, which his sister cut into fettuccine noodles. Kate and her husband are the owners of their own fixer-upper now. Just like me, she didn't show it to her mother before she bought it, and just like my mother, I asked her, "But why *that* house?" For truly, I would never have taken it on. You can see the punch line coming—it's a thing of beauty now, and as Kate hung the long strands of pasta on our old sweater-drying rack, she told us stories about their renovation, and the kitchen filled with words and laughter.

WHEN WE FINALLY SAT down to eat, there were so many of us it took three tables: one in the living room, one in the dining room, and one in the sunroom—the room we'd finally added on a few years ago, restoring symmetry to the house. We'd opened up that west wall and found the doorframe waiting. The sunroom has walls of multipane windows, just like the old back porch, and French doors that open to the dining room. As I put down a bowl of pasta on the table in the living room, I looked back through the series of rooms, one after another and out to the world beyond. It made me feel like anything was possible.

We ate slowly, course after course, until we could eat no more. Chairs were pushed back, elbows brought forward, conversations lobbed from one room to the next. Old friends rediscovered one another again, while new friendships grew roots. It had been decades since I had sat at a table in Italy and watched a family pass food and affection down its length. I could still remember what it felt like to want that. It had taken a long, long time to build and grow into this space, this house—but in that moment, sitting around our table, it felt as if we had finally come home.

The whole thing reminded me of a tradition practiced by the Zafimaniry people, who live in Madagascar. For the Zafimaniry, a house and a marriage are indeed one thing, and grow together. A couple starts with a bamboo house, built when they agree to marry. Slowly over time, wood takes the place of bamboo, and the house "acquires bones," as they say. By the end, the structure is entirely made of wood, decorated, loved right down to the details. The ultimate renovation, a physical embodiment of the care and work it takes to create a home or a relationship.

This is our Zafimaniry house. If you'd told me the day we found it that it would take almost twenty years to get to where I wanted to be, I would have said you were crazy, or perhaps more likely, I'd have run screaming from the mere thought of such an expanse of time. But one of the things an old house can teach you is that time is not the enemy of beauty—in fact, it's often quite the opposite. Time is what gives a plaster wall its luminous glow and softens the wood of a banister into the shape of your palm. Time is what gets you past the first rush of love and into the parts that actually sustain you. And time gives you the chance to gather perspective, to see your life from the altitude of experience—a blueprint, continually subject to change.

I'm not done with that process; with any luck, none of us are. This is how we move forward—one house, one tradition, one generation at a time. It takes vision and hope and not a little naivete, but in the end, we can make something beautiful. Useful. Strong.

ACKNOWLEDGMENTS

THIS BOOK HAS BEEN a long time in the making, growing and changing as I have. It took a crew to renovate our house, and it has taken another one to bring this book to light.

So thank you—to Amy Berkower and Genevieve Gagne-Hawes of Writers House, and my editor at Sasquatch, Hannah Elnan, who gave this book the gift of time to evolve and the perfect home once it did. To Jennie Shortridge, who told me to think about writing essays. To Nina Meierding, who read every draft, and my mother, who read all but the last one. And most of all to Ben, who encouraged me to write this book even when our memories differed—you are my bones.

A writer with a community has been given a gift beyond measure. The insights of Holly Smith, Bill Meierding, Michael Bauermeister, and Antoinette Mongelli always got me thinking. The women of my writing groups—Marjorie Osterhout, Thea Cooper, Randy Sue Coburn, Tara Austen Weaver, and Jennie Shortridge—have been the living definition of support. The Seattle7Writers and PT5 are my village. Carol Cassella gave me mountains and wildflowers when a deadline was fast approaching. Hedgebrook has become the North Star of my writing practice. And this book would not have happened at all if it had not been for a month spent in a residency with Aspen Words—thank you forever to Adrienne Brodeur, Marie Chan, Jamie Kravitz, and Elizabeth Nix, and a shout-out to Barbara Reese, who showed me a truth window, and Harry Teague, who set my mind spinning. And to my wonderful hosts, Isa and Daniel Shaw, who gave me a valley of golden trees and four weeks of peace and friendship—this one's for you.

As you may have noticed, the ideas in this book come from a wide range of sources, and I owe a debt of gratitude to all the authors in the bibliography. But books have to find their way to you, and I owe an equally large debt to the independent booksellers who so often put just the right book into my hands. Moonraker Books on Whidbey Island started it all by introducing me to Christopher Alexander. Deon Stonehouse of Sunriver Books in Oregon handed me *The Meaning of Home*. Imprint Books in Port Townsend was an endless source of shed inspiration. In Seattle, I discovered *Atlas Obscura* at Queen Anne Books, and visiting the architecture section at Elliott Bay Books was like opening a treasure chest, every time. And then there's Peter Miller Books, an entire bookstore dedicated to architecture and design— pretty much heaven for a house lover.

Long before there was a book, there was a house. I've been changing the names of people all along, so, alas, I cannot write the real ones here—but this book is a raised glass to all who helped bring our home back to life. Our real estate agent, who showed tenacity and creativity, even if our house scared her to death. Our architect, who continues to open my mind in so many directions. Our inspector, who didn't say we were crazy. Our three different crews, who took away the bad and built the good, giving us a house, a writing studio, a sunroom. You were, to a person, patient and good-humored and remarkably skilled, and every time a door clicks perfectly into place, we smile and think of you.

But before any of this, there were my children. It is a strange thing to have a mother who falls in love with a house. So thank you, my sweethearts. For sledgehammering and hauling trash, for listening to all the stories, and supporting me in telling mine. But most of all, for going along for the ride. I love you.

BIBLIOGRAPHY

Alexander, Christopher. *Timeless Way of Building*. New York: Oxford University Press, 1979.

Balbes, Xorin. *SoulSpace: Transform Your Home, Transform Your Life*. Novato, CA: New World Library, 2011.

Becker, Joshua. "21 Surprising Statistics That Reveal How Much Stuff We Actually Own." BecomingMinimalist.com.

Brand, Stewart. *How Buildings Learn: What Happens After They're Built*. New York: Penguin, 1994.

Bryson, Bill. *At Home: A Short History of Private Life*. New York: Doubleday, 2010.

Burton, Virginia Lee. *The Little House*. Boston: Houghton Mifflin Harcourt, 1942.

———. *Mike Mulligan and His Steam Shovel*. Boston: Houghton Mifflin Harcourt, 1939.

Cary, John. *Design for Good: A New Era of Architecture for Everyone*. Washington, DC: Island Press, 2017.

"A Conversation with Malcolm Gladwell." In the reading group guide for *Blink: The Power of Thinking Without Thinking* by Malcolm Gladwell. New York: Back Bay Books, 2007.

Daniels, Cora Linn, and C. M. Stevans (eds.). *Encyclopaedia of Superstitions, Folklore, and the Occult Sciences of the World*. Chicago: J. H. Yewdale & Sons, 1903.

de Botton, Alain. *The Architecture of Happiness*. New York: Vintage, 2006.

Durrell, Lawrence. *Spirit of Place: Letters and Essays on Travel.* London: Faber & Faber, 1969.

Eckstut, Joann, and Arielle Eckstut. *The Secret Language of Color: Science, Nature, History, Culture, Beauty of Red, Orange, Yellow, Green, Blue & Violet.* New York: Black Dog & Leventhal, 2013.

Ets, Marie Hall. *Play with Me.* New York: Viking Press, 1955.

Finlay, Victoria. *Color: A Natural History of the Palette.* New York: Random House, 2002.

Flanders, Judith. *The Making of Home: The 500-Year Story of How Our Houses Became Our Homes.* New York: Thomas Dunne Books, 2014.

Foer, Joshua, Dylan Thuras, and Ella Morton. *Atlas Obscura: An Explorer's Guide to the World's Hidden Wonders.* New York: Workman, 2016.

Frost, Randy O., and Gail Steketee. *Stuff: Compulsive Hoarding and the Meaning of Things.* Boston: Mariner Books, 2011.

Frost, Natasha. "Marvel at Tiny, Perfect Staircases Made by a Secret Society of French Woodworkers." AtlasObscura.com, March 14, 2018.

Gallagher, Winifred. *House Thinking: A Room-by-Room Look at How We Live.* New York: HarperCollins, 2006.

———. *The Power of Place: How Our Surroundings Shape Our Thoughts, Emotions, and Actions.* New York: HarperCollins, 2007.

Garber, Marjorie. *Sex and Real Estate: Why We Love Houses.* New York: Pantheon, 2000.

Goldhagen, Sarah Williams. *Welcome to Your World: How the Built Environment Shapes Our Lives.* New York: HarperCollins, 2017.

Gottman, John, and Nan Silver. *The Seven Principles for Making Marriage Work: A Practical Guide from the Country's Foremost Relationship Expert.* New York: Harmony Books, 2015.

Heathcote, Edwin. *The Meaning of Home*. London: Frances Lincoln, 2012.

Hirsch, William J., Jr. *Designing Your Perfect House: Lessons from an Architect*. Cary, NC: Dalsimer Press, 2008.

Huxtable, Ada Louise. *Frank Lloyd Wright: A Life*. New York: Penguin, 2008.

Jacobson, Max, with Shelley Brock. *Invitation to Architecture: Discovering Delight in the World Built Around Us*. Newtown, CT: Taunton, 2014.

Jacobson, Max, Murray Silverstein, and Barbara Winslow. *Patterns of Home: The Ten Essentials of Enduring Design*. Newtown, CT: Taunton, 2002.

Ketcherside, Rob. *Lost Seattle*. London: Pavilion Books, 2013.

Kondo, Marie. *The Life-Changing Magic of Tidying Up: The Japanese Art of Decluttering and Organizing*. Berkeley: Ten Speed, 2014.

Lurie, Alison. *The Language of Houses: How Buildings Speak to Us*. New York: Delphinium Books, 2014.

Marcus, Clare Cooper. *House as a Mirror of Self: Exploring the Deeper Meaning of Home*. Lake Worth, FL: Nicolas-Hays, 2006.

May, John. *Buildings without Architects: A Global Guide to Everyday Architecture*. New York: Rizzoli, 2010.

McAlpine, Bobby, and Susan Ferrier. *Art of the House: Reflections on Design*. New York: Rizzoli, 2014.

Moore, Rowan. *Why We Build: Power and Desire in Architecture*. New York: HarperCollins, 2013.

Morgan, Murray. *The Last Wilderness*. Seattle: University of Washington Press, 1976.

Murphy, Michael. "Architecture That's Built to Heal." TED Talk, February 2016.

Nash, George. *Renovating Old Houses.* Newtown, CT: Taunton, 1998.

Owen, David. *The Walls Around Us: The Thinking Person's Guide to How a House Works.* New York: Villard Books, 1991.

Plante, Ellen M. *The American Kitchen: 1700 to Present.* New York: Facts On File, 1995.

Pollan, Michael. *A Place of My Own: The Education of an Amateur Builder.* New York: Random House, 1997.

Rasmussen, Steen Eiler. *Experiencing Architecture.* Cambridge: MIT Press, 1959.

Rybczynski, Witold. *Home: A Short History of an Idea.* New York: Viking, 1986.

————. *The Most Beautiful House in the World.* New York: Penguin, 1990.

Sarton, May. *Plant Dreaming Deep.* New York: W. W. Norton, 1968.

Sayer, Liana C. "Trends in Women's and Men's Time Use, 1965–2012: Back to the Future?" In *Gender and Couple Relationships,* edited by Susan M. McHale, Valerie King, Jennifer Van Hook, and Alan Booth. New York: Springer, 2015.

Sholl, Jessie. *Dirty Secret: A Daughter Comes Clean About Her Mother's Compulsive Hoarding.* New York: Gallery Books, 2011.

Shirley, Frank. *New Rooms for Old Houses: Beautiful Additions for the Traditional Home.* Newtown, CT: Taunton, 2007.

Speck, Jeff. "The Walkable City." TED Talk, September 2013.

St. Clair, Kassia. *The Secret Lives of Color.* New York: Penguin, 2017.

Staten, Vince. *Did Monkeys Invent the Monkey Wrench?: Hardware Stores and Hardware Stories.* New York: Touchstone, 1997.

Susanka, Sarah. *Creating the Not So Big House*. Newtown, CT: Taunton, 2000.

———. *Home by Design: Transforming Your House into Home*. Newtown, CT: Taunton, 2004.

Sussman, Ann, and Justin Hollander. *Cognitive Architecture*. New York: Routledge, 2014.

Thoreau, Henry David. *Walden*. London: Orion, 1995.

Too, Lillian. *The Complete Illustrated Guide to Feng Shui*. Rockport, MA: Element Books, 1997.

Weston, Richard. *100 Ideas That Changed Architecture*. London: Laurence King, 2011.

Woolf, Virginia. *A Room of One's Own*. New York: Harcourt, 2005.

ABOUT THE AUTHOR

ERICA BAUERMEISTER is the bestselling author of four novels: *The School of Essential Ingredients, Joy for Beginners, The Lost Art of Mixing,* and *The Scent Keeper.* Before she turned to fiction, she was the coauthor of two readers' guides: *500 Great Books by Women* and *Let's Hear It For the Girls.* She lives in Port Townsend, Washington, with her husband and 238 deer.